HEALING THE FISHER KING

A FLY FISHER'S GRAIL QUEST

G. SCOTT SPARROW

Also by G. Scott Sparrow

Lucid Dreaming: Dawning of the Clear Light (ARE Press)

*I Am with You Always: True Stories of Encounters
with Jesus (Bantam, 1994)*

*Blessed Among Women: Encounters with Mary and Her Message
(Crown, 1997)*

Sacred Encounters with Jesus (Ave Maria, 2002)

Saved Encounters with Mary (Ave Maria, 2003)

The Blue Ornament (BlueMantle, 2015)

HEALING THE FISHER KING

A FLY FISHER'S GRAIL QUEST

G. SCOTT SPARROW

BlueMantle
United States of America

For Chas Matthews

Acknowledgments

This book recounts a journey encompassing over seven years, but recollects, as well, some of my earliest memories in deep South Texas. Consequently, there are many people who assisted me along the way, many of whom must regrettably go unmentioned. I often marvel at the adventures that my buddy Roger Nolen and I shared during our youth, and I give him immense credit for pushing me, for better or worse, beyond my known horizons as an angler and as a young man. I also owe a great deal of thanks to Capt. Skipper Ray, Larry Haines, and Bud Rowland — fellow members of the Laguna Madre Fly Fishing Association — who generously shared with me their knowledge of fly fishing for giant speckled trout; my brother Chip, his son Spencer, and my fly fishing buddies Bill May, Cecil Marchant, Henry Bone, and Joe MacKay, who provided a precious source of male companionship in my development as a fly fisher and guide; and video guru Jeff Pill of Miracle Productions, whose mentoring has been an invaluable source of guidance.

Several of my non-fishing mentors and friends played important roles in helping me to awaken to the spiritual dimensions of my life. In that regard, I am thankful for the soul-level companionship of Bobbi Kay Jones, Hugh Lynn Cayce, Herbert Puryear, Henry Reed, Mark Thurston, Giles Nowak, and Michael Reidy.

My father's support was always there, too — with his lifelong enthusiasm for fishing the Lower Laguna and his wholly uncritical attitude toward my various ventures. I owe so much, as well, to my son Ryan who supported my relocation to South Texas, in spite of the geographical distance that it put between us.

Contents

Preface

This is not principally a book about fly fishing, nor about catching fish. It is about the rift between the mind and the heart in the souls of men, and the process that can make us whole again.

We would like to think that every good story has a clear beginning and end. While that may be possible in fiction, it is rarely true in the course of a person's genuine spiritual awakening and maturation. Between the singular frame of birth and death, we encounter endlessly repeating themes — and, if we persist, we make some progress toward the resolution of those patterns that impede the full expression of the soul. Indeed, our most important lessons repeat themselves over and over until there arises sufficient insight and commitment to sustain a new pattern of living in the face of habit. Spiritual enlightenment, at least from this standpoint, is not a fixed state of awareness into which error can no longer insinuate itself. It is the dynamic capacity to reaffirm, on a moment-to-moment basis, the highest that we know to be true, without falling prey to unthinking reactions based on fear and illusion. From this perspective, enlightenment is more of a yoke than a mantle.

In telling a good story, there is a fine line between creativity and deception. Walking that line, we may reorder the facts and fit them neatly into a convenient time frame. Some of this, I believe, is acceptable, as long as we do not lead the reader to think that the story is over when it's not. For the consequences of such deception would be to instill expectations in the reader that cannot be quickly realized in anyone's life.

This is all to say that my fly fishing quest on my home waters in the summer of 1997 provided a convenient time frame for telling most, but not all of the story. My retreat to the Lower Laguna Madre served as a powerful catalyst for awakening me to patterns in my life that impeded my ability to live fully, and it provided a context for working through many of these problems.

i

The climax of the story revolves around a broken promise — one among many in the course of my life — and the consequences that ensued. It provides a dramatic example of what can befall us when we persist in turning away from our deepest calling, but it also shows how the inevitable ensuing crisis can precipitate a veritable "turning about in the deepest seat of consciousness," and inaugurate a new pattern of living informed by the heart. Since this crisis was eerily foreshadowed by my experiences during my fly fishing retreat in 1997, and became a life and death matter for me five years later, it seemed fitting to bring this culminating event into the whole picture.

Each chapter segment is comprised of a brief entry recounting events of the summer of 2002, and the chapter itself covering the period from early 1997 until the end my retreat to the Lower Laguna Madre in August 1997.

G. Scott Sparrow
Arroyo City, Texas
January 2009

The Story of the Fisher King

Once upon a time, there is a young prince named Amfortas, who rides his horse into the woods one day looking for an opportunity to test his knightly skills. Encountering no one, he grows hungry toward the end of the day and goes looking for something to eat. He chances upon a campsite where he finds a salmon cooking over an open fire. Without inquiring into  *the fish's ownership, he seizes a piece of the salmon to eat, only to find that it is much too hot to handle. It burns his hand and his mouth, wounding him terribly. In another version of the story, the fish's owner returns and shoots an arrow that lodges between the thief's testicles. In still a third version, Amfortas encounters a pagan knight returning from the Holy Land. Eager to prove himself, Amfortas charges the stranger. The men fight until Amfortas kills the pagan knight — but not before the knight succeeds in castrating the impetuous prince.*

Regardless of the source of his wound, Amfortas can not heal. Languishing in his castle, he awaits the coming of a peerless knight, whose willing service to the Grail will win Amfortas deliverance from his pain. He is thereafter called the Fisher King because fishing is the only thing that gives him relief from his torment.

Years later, an innocent youth named Parcifal sets about to become a knight. Unbeknownst to him, he is the one destined to find and serve the Grail, and to end the Fisher King's suffering.

A Disturbing Dream

> *A stingray lay unmoving at my feet in the shallow, clear water. Before I could move out of its way, it transformed into a man of stone and began to attack me. Sensing that he intended to kill me, I desperately defended myself and eventually prevailed, but only after chipping away at him, piece by piece, until there was nothing left of him.*

Three days after the dream, almost to the minute, my alarm clock sounded at 4 a.m.

I got out of bed and went upstairs to awaken my friend Tim Clancey and my son, Ryan. The first day of the 64th annual Texas International Fishing Tournament (TIFT) would commence at sunrise, and I intended for us to be on the water, ready to fish, by first light. Tim had come down from San Antonio to compete with me in the tournament, and Ryan — who had only recently begun to fly fish — had decided to go along and help us with the boat. It was a "kill" tournament — one in which the contestants take dead fish to a weigh-in — and I'd promised myself never to fish one again. But when Tim expressed interest in fishing together, I decided to fish the TIFT one last time.

The night before, I had become obsessed with the idea of staking out a place called the Trout Bar — my favorite big trout venue — before the other contestants arrived. Having won the TIFT fly fishing division the first time I entered it two years before, I knew that catching a big trout was the key to winning. As I rushed around in the wee hours of morning packing gear and grabbing a bit of breakfast, I failed to visit the bathroom — an omission that can ruin my day.

It was so dark when we left the dock that we had to use a Q-beam to guide us on our eight-mile journey. Even with the searchlight's help, I overshot our destination and had to circle back to locate the

1

exact spot. Planing onto the edge of the flat, I turned off the motor and poled quietly into an area that's famous among local anglers for hosting the largest speckled trout in the bay — if not the world. Meanwhile, the running lights from several boats could be seen approaching from the south. We had arrived first, and the Trout Bar was ours.

It was against TIFT rules to begin fishing before sunrise, so we spent some time preparing our gear and joking around. Ryan was in rare form, obviously excited to be a part of "the team." Then, feeling the urge to relieve myself before the tournament began, I stepped off the boat and waded toward a nearby spoil island.

Ryan asked, "Where are you going, Dad?"

"To the men's room," I replied.

He began to make fun of me, but I knew if I didn't follow through, I'd be miserable later. As I approached the south island of the Trout Bar, the black skimmers and black-necked stilts that were nesting there began squawking and hovering overhead as I searched for the largest black mangrove to crouch beside, as if anyone could see me in the twilight. Burying the evidence of my intrusion under a pile of dead seagrass, I started back toward the boat. Instead of wading carefully, I moved quickly — deep in thought and eager to begin the day.

My thoughts centered on finding and catching big trout, instead of attending to the task at hand. Distracted by that singular aim, I took a step, and when my right foot came down, I felt a sharp, stabbing pain that quickly rose to almost intolerable levels.

"Oh God!" I yelled. It felt like a hot knife had sliced through my ankle, leaving behind the signature of something coldly impersonal. I could barely keep walking, as almost immediately my leg muscles locked up from the pain.

"What happened?" Tim yelled, with alarm in his voice.

"A stingray got me!" I yelled bacKathy

Tim and Ryan piled out of the boat and came to assist me. As I stood there waiting for them, I realized that the stingray's wound had been foreshadowed by the ominous dream three days before and by a number of other dreams, as well. Indeed, a series of experiences be-

ginning in 1996 pointed to my return to my home waters and to an en-counter with an stingray.

The year of 1996 proved to be a particularly difficult time. I had left my marriage two years before, and my seven-year-old son lived a mile away with his mother. Meanwhile, I had pursued a new relationship that was doomed from the outset and eventually came to a nightmarish end in the late summer. I recall sitting at my dining room table, talking to a Virginia Beach policeman, who was 20 years my junior, but wise enough to ask the obvious question, "Why do you let her back in?" I replied, of course, "Because I love her." But I discovered, as so many of us are destined to learn in time, that love is not always enough.

Free, at last, from the turmoil, but not the grief of ending that relationship, I visited bars almost nightly, and I drank too much beer on too many occasions before admitting the futility of that empty source of solace. After my friend Giles voiced his concern, I consented at last to spending my nights at home, sober and alone. By day I was a therapist, helping others. By night, I felt broken and invisible.

On a cold evening in mid-January 1997, I took the first tentative step in my journey homeward by beginning to reminisce about the place where my father had taken me fishing when I was a child — the Lower Laguna Madre of deep South Texas.

Of all of the places I had known, it alone called to me.

1

The Mother Lagoon

Virginia Beach — January 1997

"The phenomenon itself, that is, the vision of light, is an experience common to many mystics, and one that is undoubtedly of the greatest significance, because in all times and places it appears as the unconditional thing, which unites in itself the greatest energy and the profoundest meaning." [1]

Carl Jung

When Jesus chose his first disciples, he selected several men who had fished for a living. People who do not fish may consider this fact irrelevant. But those of us who do fish — if only for sport — and who enjoy the companionship of others who do, can imagine what Jesus might have seen in the likes of Peter, James, John, and Andrew. For the dream of catching a big fish is not unlike the dream of communing with God: The fisherman and the mystic alike are driven by a yearning for something elusive and essential just below the surface of ordinary life. Whether we think of it as a great fish or as God himself who beckons us onward in our quest, it feels remarkably the same.

Some of my first memories on the Gulf Coast of South Texas are of blue crabs and piggy perch, and of my father untangling my fishing line, again and again, on the dock below the cottage. Dad was always patient, and looking back, I realize now that this was his gift to me.

---

[1] Wilhelm, R. 1962. *The Secret of the Golden Flower.* New York: Harcourt, Brace and World.

4

We lived 45 miles inland, but we spent many of our summer weekends at the cottage on the Arroyo Colorado. Dad had "inherited" the cottage from my mother's entrepreneurial father who had suffered a financial setback and could not afford to keep up the payments. So Dad, who would never have bought such a place for himself, took it over for several years until his penchant for self-denial under the guise of prudence prompted him to sell it for $4,000. I can remember that for many years afterward — as we launched our boat from the public launch like everybody else and boated past Arroyo City toward the bay — we would try to pick out from among the assortment of vacation homes the cottage that had once been ours.

The Arroyo Colorado was once the riverbed of the Rio Grande River. It begins as a mere trickle 70 miles inland, at the point where the Rio Grande broke away centuries ago and followed a more southerly course. By the time the Arroyo reaches Arroyo City, it is over 100 yards wide and looks like a substantial river. Five miles east, it enters the Lower Laguna Madre — a shallow hypersaline estuary that lies between the mainland of South Texas and Padre Island. From the point where the Arroyo enters the estuary, the Lower Laguna extends about 40 miles to the north and 20 miles to the south. Encompassing nearly 300 square-miles of sand flats and grassy lagoons, the Lower Laguna is remarkable for its primitive and unmarred beauty. It reveals itself as a spacious expanse of clear water, and it is the largest continuous shallow-water flat in the North America.

Circumstances have conspired to protect the Lower Laguna from the encroachment of modern life. One of the largest ranches in the United States — the King Ranch — claims much of the western shoreline of the estuary northward from the Arroyo. And then, to the south, the Laguna Atascosa National Wildlife Refuge insulates the shoreline for another 15 miles. Consequently, the Lower Laguna Madre remains one of the last remaining primitive estuaries in the world. Except for a few fishing huts on stilts, there is absolutely nothing unnatural to see, except for an occasional barge on its way somewhere, or a small boat that seems lost in the expanse of water and sky.

As a child, I knew nothing of the Laguna Madre's secrets, nor of its beauty. My father's plywood V-bottom boat could only travel in the channels created by dredging, which limited our range of exploration considerably. We were restricted in our fishing to the murky, manmade channel called the Intracoastal Waterway that slices unnaturally through the Laguna Madre from north to south, permitting deep-draft vessels to pass safely through the estuary.

Back then, we would leave the dock at daybreak, and travel eastward five miles to the mouth of the Arroyo. We would stop and buy live shrimp from an old gentleman who lived in a hut on stilts, and whose loss of his larynx to cancer made him a man of a few whispered words. My father, whose responsibilities to his family always prevented him from pursuing the dream of a simpler life, often had something good to say about this man who lived so simply on the edge of the bay, and who could be so generous with his shrimp. At the mouth of the Arroyo, we would intersect the 50-yard-wide Intracoastal channel, and turning north or south, we would find a place to anchor along its edges. There we would cast live shrimp on treble hooks back into the deeper water and wait for the bobber — which we properly called a "cork" regardless of its composition — to disappear.

For years, we caught innumerable spotted or "speckled" trout that way, so there never seemed to be a reason to go elsewhere or to innovate. But every once in a while, we'd see something that made us wonder. A tiny boat would pass us by to the east, skimming over water that was only a foot or so deep. These homemade plywood "scooters" were, essentially, wide flat-bottomed skis powered by outboard motors. When they would come to the dock, their captains — whom I remember as kind, but tightlipped old timers — would unload huge trout and redfish, the likes of which we had never seen at the end of our lines. Denial is a powerful thing, so somehow we kept explaining such miracles away until, in the face of the evidence, my brother began to wonder out loud what secrets the spacious shallow waters would reveal if only we could go there. But my dad, whose strong suit was consistency, was content to do what we'd always done. It was years before my brother and I left the old ways behind. When we did, we took our father with us.

At the center of this watery universe lay an island that I never once visited as a child. From the first time I saw Green Island, I felt drawn to go there. Flocks of terns, herons, and egrets made Green Island their home. An occasional peregrine falcon could be seen circling over the island — probably calculating the risk of making a kill amongst so many sharp beaks. It was a place that was teeming with life and shrouded in mystery. Roseate spoonbills, also island residents, lined the southern shoreline and looked like a string of pearls around a impenetrable wall of green. No one I knew had ever stepped foot on Green Island. Today, it is an Audubon bird sanctuary and off limits to casual visitors, but back then, there was  apparently nothing standing in the way of its exploration except shallow water and indifference.

I would sometimes ask Dad if we could go there. When he explained that there was an impassable expanse of shallow water between us and the island, I would gaze at it longingly, imagining all of the things that might be found there. The tree-covered island was almost always somewhere within my view — if only as a thin green line on the horizon — and it worked on me continuously to awaken a yearning that would assume many forms later in my life.

In time, I came to feel completely at home on the Laguna Madre. As we would speed eastward toward the bay in the morning twilight, I would dangle my legs over the bow of the boat, gripping the bow line like a bronco rider and relishing the warm, humid summer air flowing over me. The pervasive smell of fish — both living and dead, the cool pockets of air left over from the night, and the occasional howl of a coyote roaming the tidal flats — each familiar sensation greeted me as part of a rich, expansive experience of arriving at the one place most precious to me in all of the world.

I have since discovered that fly fishermen, in particular, often speak with a deep reverence for their "home waters." The place itself does not have to be the best place to fish, nor even notable in that regard: But it is where — over time and by degrees — a fisherman acquires an intimacy with nature and a mastery of his sport. And above all, it is where he comes to feel most at home in the world.

The recurrent experience of one's home waters can become central to one's spiritual life by intimating the possibility of an enduring state of inner harmony. Indeed, just as the fisherman's desire for a great fish parallels the fervor of the mystic in his yearning for God, the fisherman's experience of his home waters is not unlike the mystic's experience of arriving at his destination. My initial experience of what the mystics refer to as the Holy Light, for instance, made me aware of how heaven must feel just like home — and how, in turn, one's true home must feel just like heaven.

I had just turned 19, and was away from home for the first time as a freshman at the University of Texas in Austin. The experience began as an ordinary dream in which I was returning home from my college classes, carrying my books. As I approached my home, which bore no resemblance whatsoever to my actual home or dormitory, I realized suddenly that I was dreaming. I looked at my body and was amazed at how real everything seemed. Marveling at this paradox, I approached large black double-doors with ornate brass handles and opened them. As soon as I did, intense white light poured into my being, lifting me into an exquisite sense of love and joy that I'd never known. I entered the small room, which appeared to be a chapel. The white light bathed everything, and the sense of being home was total and complete. At one point, I carried a crystal rod upright, over which a spinning circle of crystal was poised in midair. No one was there to explain the mystery of the light, or the immense purpose that I felt.

Even today, when I think about this experience, I can feel something of what I felt then — so totally fulfilled and so completely at home. Sparse Gray Hackle, author of *Fishless Days and Angling Nights*[2] has said, "Sometimes I think the least important thing about fishing is catching fish." He never says, however, what the most important thing about fishing is. Like the Hindu meditator who evokes the experience of the Divine by repeating the mantric words *neti, neti* — not this, not that — he says that fishing is really about something that cannot be easily named. As a fisherman matures on his home waters, this becomes increasingly clear. Indeed, I think that all great anglers eventually realize what the great mystics have always known — that the fulfillment of the quest is never exactly what you expect it to be. And while the true goal cannot be easily named, we know when we are drawing close to it when we begin to feel completely at home in the world.

My transformation from a bait fisherman on the Intracoastal Waterway to a fly fisherman on the adjoining "flats" of the Lower Laguna Madre took place in steps over many years.

When I was 14, my scout troop participated in an area-wide Boy Scout fishing tournament. We camped in army tents on South Padre Island and fished for two days in the Laguna Madre. None of the hundred or so scouts knew how to fish the shallow waters of the estuary, so since I had only fished with bait in the deeper Intracoastal Waterway, my best friend Roger and I employed my father's time-tested methods. We bought some shrimp, waded out into the bay, and proceeded to get frustrated as the piggy perch and catfish picked us clean. On the second day, however, I somehow managed to catch a three-pound sheepshead — a marginal game fish, at best — which turned out to be the largest fish caught during the two-day tournament. On the

---

2 Hackle, S. G. 1971. *Fishless Days and Angling Nights*. New York: Crown.

basis of this single fish, I won the individual trophy and my troop won the overall trophy. As we were preparing to leave, trophies in hand, a couple of the sponsors of the tournament — who had waded north of the camp early that morning — returned on foot, dragging behind them several large trout and redfish. The iridescent hues of the big trout, in particular, mesmerized me, and I was suddenly willing to do whatever it took to have that fish on the end of my line. When I asked one of the men what he had used for bait, he told me politely that he had used artificial lures, not bait at all. Chastened by his greater knowledge, I vowed that, in time, I would learn his secrets.

I obtained my driver's license soon afterward, so I began driving to South Padre Island to fish. My brother was away flying jets in the Air Force at that time, so my early exploration of the bay was largely a solitary affair. I would drive 50 miles to the causeway which connects Port Isabel to South Padre Island, drive up the island, and then wade westward into the shallow Laguna. I'd taught myself to fly fish several years earlier, but it had not yet occurred to me or anyone else I knew that the Lower Laguna was a fly fisher's paradise. So, using an old eight-foot fly rod that had been converted to a spinning rod — to increase the distance that I could cast — I would cast small gold spoons to tailing redfish and black drum, and blindly pick up an occasional speckled trout. I was still pretty ignorant, but my sheer enthusiasm accounted for early successes.

By the late '60s, my father's friend, Kenny Barth had become something of a legend as a shallow-water fisherman. In addition to other notable accomplishments, he had caught an unprecedented 27-pound redfish on light spin tackle in a foot of water. While wading one afternoon off of South Padre Island, Kenny had seen the big fish's back out of the water. Using a converted fly rod outfitted with a tiny spinning reel, he quickly cast a gold spoon to it. Never content to cast ordinary lures to his fish, Kenny had painted the back side of the lure with his secret weapon — the color "cerise," otherwise known as hot pink on the street. Whether the pink flash made any difference or not, the big fish devoured the lure nonetheless. As Kenny prepared to watch all of his eight-pound test line unwind, the 42-inch fish panicked and swam into even shallower water! Kenny, who understood that a miracle was in the making, promptly dropped his rod and jumped on the fish before it could return to deeper water. They struggled in the shallow water before the larger of the two emerged the victor. Kenny's

reputation as one of the master fishermen in the Lower Laguna Madre was cemented by this unprecedented fishing feat and was supported for years thereafter by the abundant fishing tales that issued from his willing lips.

Anyone who fishes the "skinny water" of the Laguna Madre — where redfish rarely grow to more than 15 pounds before leaving the bay — can testify that Kenny's catch on such light tackle was a feat of inconceivable proportions. Larger redfish can be found in the open Gulf and Atlantic from Texas to Virginia. But the Laguna Madre is, strictly speaking, a nursery for juvenile redfish destined for the spawning grounds of the open Gulf.

Norman Maclean, author of *A River Runs Through It,*[3] has said, "All good things come by grace, and grace comes by art, and art does not come easy." In considering Kenny's obvious experience of grace, we might ask, Where was the art? The thought of Kenny face down in a foot of water with a fish in his arms doesn't exactly inspire poetry. But I have come to believe that Kenny's bold technique is more the rule than the exception when it comes to the pivotal moments of our lives. I believe that most master fishermen would probably agree that the importance of art diminishes considerably as miracles unfold, and that grace becomes strangely responsive to the artless, sheer determination to win the prize, even if it means leaping upon it. Perhaps that is why we have so many stories in the Bible where bold opportunism, and nothing else, wins God's favor. Perhaps men like Kenny, who might seem to employ overly crude tactics, elicit respect and humor in the mind and heart of God.

In this vein, there is a story in a modern science fiction work[4], in which a man and his wife are preparing to leave the planet where they have lived for some time. The wife sends her lazy husband to obtain a suitable rocket for their departure. As he rummages through the assortment of vessels, he carelessly chooses one that will explode and kill them. At that moment, a being appears to him, informs him that his choice will prove fatal, and advises him to choose another rocket. Recognizing the being as the Walker — a manifestation of God — the grateful man asks, "But why? What have I done?" He knows full well that he hasn't done much to merit God's grace. The Walker asks him if he remembers his favorite pet — a tomcat — that had died choking on a buzzard bone. The man then remembers with great fondness the totally incorrigible animal that he had loved so much for his sheer passion and spirit.

The Walker says, "You would have paid a great deal to have him alive again, but you would have wanted him as he was, greedy and pushy, himself as you loved him, unchanged. Do you understand?"

---

[3] MacLean, N. 1976. *A River Runs Through It.* Chicago: University of Chicago.

[4] Phillip DicKathy 1970. *A Maze of Death.* New York: Doubleday.

It was not long before Kenny heard about my novice exploits, and he let my father know that he would like me to join him some weekend at his mobile home on Padre Island. I was puzzled by this man's attention, for I had only met him in passing. Having no words at the time to describe a budding mentoring relationship, I nonetheless felt something of immense importance in his invitation, so I made plans to join him one Friday afternoon after worKathy Because my father and Kenny were close friends, Dad gave me Saturday off from my job and wished me the best of lucKathy

I arrived at Kenny's trailer just before dark and found him preparing the food for the weekend. His menu consisted almost exclusively of beans and steamed shrimp, and he had cooked huge pots of each to sustain us through the stay. He welcomed me like we were old friends, and he proceeded to talk incessantly about fishing lures, secret fishing places, and the many fish that he had recently caught.

Kenny talked a lot but did not seem to listen very much: He simply had too much to tell me. I have since concluded that a good mentor does not have to listen very well, but he needs to know what you need to know and how to impart this wisdom. Robert Bly has observed that male initiation is usually performed by uncles and men who are not our fathers, because our fathers are much too attached to the outcome. Kenny knew what I needed to know, he knew how to teach me, and he expressed no attachment to my success. Actually, he was always slightly competitive — as most fishermen are — with anyone who might outfish him.

The first night I spent at Kenny's island trailer, I dreamt of the deeper meaning behind his invitation. In the dream, I found myself standing outside the trailer. Nearby was a large circular building, which I knew was a temple. As I entered the building, I went before an altar, upon which a giant golden fish stood on its tail, which I knew to be a symbol for God. I was filled with a sense of meaning and I awoke.

It was a rainy weekend, but Kenny and I fished as we much as we could. We drove up and down Padre Island in his old Wagoneer, listened endlessly to the same worn tape of Henry Mancini playing on his eight-track player, and picked up trash that other people had care-lessly thrown on the beach. We examined things that I, alone, would have overlooked in my headlong pursuit of narrowly defined goals. Somehow in that short time, Kenny's love for the Island and the estu-ary effectively became my own. Thomas Jefferson once said that husbandry was the core virtue of the American ideal. Looking back, I believe that Kenny awakened in me a deep sense of husbandry for the Laguna Madre.

Several months later, I was wade fishing with my brother, brother-in-law, and father at "Barth's Hole," a fishing spot on the Laguna Madre which carried Kenny's name. I had caught 11 redfish over an old oyster bed, while the others had caught only three fish between them. It was one of those magical, embarrassing days when everything

went in my favor. As we headed back to the car with a few of the red-fish in hand, Kenny and a friend of his drove up in the old Wagoneer and were star-tled to see my catch. Kenny admitted with some awk-wardness that  they had come up empty-handed. Would I, he asked, lend him three fish so he could have something to take home to Estelle? He finally confessed that he had bet his wife — who often outfished him — that he could bring home supper, and he was willing to exploit the ambigui-ties of the wager in order to win. In the spirit of supporting Kenny's bold opportunism, I gladly consented. He never repaid me with fish, but his infectious enthusiasm and his recognition of our kinship have since fed me many times times over.

Not long ago, Kenny and Estelle moved away from the bay. Estelle had become ill, and Kenny felt that they needed to be closer to medical care. When I spoke to him, perhaps for the last time, he didn't seem sad about leaving his home waters, for he was doing his duty, as he always has.

Maybe Kenny will come back someday to where he and Estelle fished for so much of their lives, and where he loved to grow flowers, papayas, and watermelons on the edge of the bay. Perhaps, I will be there to welcome him. But regardless, some things will remain the same: The Laguna Madre will always be there, and those of us who fashion ourselves her masters will come and go like the tides.

Friday, August 3, 2002, sunrise
Arroyo City, Texas

I Decide to Fish

Leaning on Tim and Ryan as I walked, I finally crawled onto the boat and with great effort removed my wading boot. Ryan shined the light on the puncture wound, which was bleeding freely. The ray's stinger had passed through the neoprene boot like it was paper and entered my foot at an angle between the ankle bone and the Achilles tendon. A red welt on the other side of my ankle announced that the stinger had stopped just short of passing all the way through. Fortunately, the barb itself did not seem to be lodged in the wound.

Tim insisted that we go in, but after considering that option, I declined the offer. He had come all the way from San Antonio to fish the TIFT, and I didn't want to ruin his chances of winning. Or mine.

"It's going to hurt no matter where I am," I said. "I'd rather deal with it out here, and fish, than sit around the house," I asserted.

I stifled a groan as I pulled the bootie back onto my foot. Ryan stayed on the boat equipped with a walkie talkie, as Tim and I slipped overboard and headed off in different directions. Every step was a monumental effort, but I gave myself pep talks and did my best to focus on fishing. Like the Fisher King in the legend of the Holy Grail — whose pain would subside only when he fished — I noticed that I could take my mind off the pain whenever I was fighting a fish. I was pleased that I could tolerate the distress, because I'd heard so many people say that the stingray's toxin was known to make grown men cry.

17

2

A Dream Calls Me Homeward

Virginia Beach — January 1997

*Life, as suffering, is the story of endless partial solutions
to an unrequited yearning for wholeness."*
Journal entry

I taught myself to fly fish when I was 12, having never seen it done, but feeling inexplicably drawn to the gracefulness of the sport. Around that time, my father and a group of his deer hunting friends leased a ranch 80 miles north of our hometown. During my first trip to the Jones' ranch, I came upon an unexpected treasure. Out in the middle of the South Texas brush country, I discovered a working windmill, whose outpouring had created a shallow, clear lake that was filled with cruising largemouth bass. With obvious premeditation, the rancher had encircled the lake with a fence, so that his watering cattle could only drink on the edges of this remarkable oasis, leaving it clear and unmolested.

Meanwhile, the voluminous Herters catalog had been captivating me with colorful pictures of delicate flies and bass bugs; so with the oasis in mind, I purchased my first fly reel from Herters for $2.95 and bought the only fly rod in stock at the local hardware store — a dusty, Garcia eight-foot fiberglass rod. Not long after, while we rested at the deer camp in the middle of the day, my father gave me a ride to the oasis and sat in the car nursing a headache while I fly fished for the first time. I stood on the edge of the clear water and caught one bass after another on tiny poppers, overcome by the ease with which I could catch fish in this delicate and simple manner. I shouted to my father to share in my discovery, but he felt so badly that he never got out of the

18

car. For Dad's sake, I cut short my first fly fishing adventure, and for some reason, I never fished the oasis again. But it didn't matter. I was a fly fisherman from that moment onward.

After my brother returned from the Air Force in the mid-70s, I introduced him to fishing the vast flats of the Laguna Madre. Having envisioned the potential for shallow water fishing years earlier, Chip was eager to join me. Soon afterward, he bought his first shallow-draft boat that could negotiate the shallow lagoons of the Lower Laguna, and we entered a new phase in our family's fishing career. A couple of years later, I took the final step in my maturation as a Laguna Madre fisherman: I began fly fishing on the bay. Once again, I was alone in my experiment. My dad's vision was too impaired to adopt the sport, and my brother — an expert spin fisherman by then — had never shown any interest in changing his methods. Regardless, after hearing rumors that a few men were experimenting with fly fishing on the bay, I took my only graphite fly rod with us one morning.

The bay was absolutely calm and shrouded in a thin fog. I have rarely encountered such profound stillness on the Laguna Madre: It was as if nature itself held still in support of my venture. I stepped quietly out of the boat in 15 inches of glassy water and began casting into the gray mist a floating deer hair fly that I had tied myself. In only minutes, I managed to catch two redfish on my seven-weight rod, both of which rose to the surface and inhaled the fly with characteristic aggression. I was ecstatic, and again, the implications seemed staggering. I expected my brother to grab the rod from me and begin casting the fly himself. But having caught nothing, he seemed only mildly interested and ready to move on. I was puzzled at his disinterest, but regardless, I put my spinning rods away for good and began to fly fish exclusively on the Lower Laguna.

When I graduated from the University of Texas in 1973, I moved to Virginia, and have lived here ever since. Since then, I have returned to my home waters each summer to fish and to commune, in particular, with my brother and father, and my friend Cecil, who — like myself — fishes exclusively with a fly rod. That yearly pilgrimage seemed just enough until recently when I passed through a particularly difficult time in my life. Since then, I have felt the overwhelming urge to return to the shores of those familiar waters for a more lengthy stay. On the surface, I fashion myself finally ready to go after a world record speckled trout on a fly rod, and I know I will have to set aside more time to realize this dream.

While my goal is admittedly ambitious, my chances of catching such a fish over the course of two months are actually quite good. Most of the largest speckled trout that have been taken on a fly rod have been caught on the east coast of Florida or on the Lower Laguna Madre. Several of the current IGFA world records, including the largest trout ever caught on a fly rod, were caught on the Lower Laguna.

The speckled trout is a member of the croaker family, and like its cousins — the redfish, the black drum, and the croaker — speckled trout range from the upper Chesapeake Bay to the Gulf Coast of Mexico. Aptly named *cynoscion nebulosus,* or "starry nebulae" for the sweep of spots that cover its iridescent back, it resembles a fresh water trout, except for its gaping mouth and two teeth.

Before they reach the spawning age of two years, and a length of about 15 inches, trout feed on shrimp and small baitfish and, while feeding, will often attack just about anything that you toss in their direction. Indeed, small topwater and subsurface flies will draw as many as a half dozen slashing strikes on a single retrieve through a school of feeding trout. However, if small trout are the easiest prey, large trout are the hardest. As they grow in size, they eventually break free of the schools and become an altogether different animal prowling the shallow flats. The largest trout are females, with the males rarely growing beyond 20 inches in size. A six year-old male will average 19 inches in length, while a six-year-old female will average 26 inches. These large "sow trout" tend to feed only two hours out of every 24-hour cycle, and when they do feed, they usually gorge themselves on baitfish such as mullet, pinfish, ballyhoo, or pigfish. In fact, it is not uncommon to find a trophy trout choking, if not already dead, with a large mullet hanging from its mouth.

While I have fished for speckled trout all my life, the quest for giant trout came into focus only recently. Catskill legend Edward R. Hewitt would have predicted this late arrival, for he once said, "First a man tries to catch the most fish, then the largest fish, and finally the most difficult fish." It is hard to say what accounts for this change of heart — whether it's an accumulation of successes, or failures, or the right amount of each — that finally takes us beyond crude quantitative measures of success. But when the change comes, there's no going bacKathy It is then when certain fish and certain dreams that have lurked vaguely on the edges of the imagination suddenly come into focus.

Even without a midlife crisis to bring this dream to life, the quest for giant trout would have happened sooner or later, for the seeds of obsession were implanted at an early age by my father, who had always regarded them with a special reverence and awe. Even today at 86, Dad imagines hearing a trout in every noisy swirl of a mullet's tail, and seeing one in every clump of floating grass. For years, my brother and I would groan inwardly at my father's fantasies. But somewhere along the way, I began to see the world as he did, and then the only things that really mattered were few in number and often beyond my reach — like difficult fish and God.

The idea of a midlife retreat on my home waters actually began as far back as 1993 through a momentous dream which pointed compellingly to the Laguna Madre as offering something that I deeply yearned for, and needed.

In the dream, I was at my childhood home in South Texas. It was late at night when I went out in the backyard and looked eastward toward the Gulf of Mexico. A warm wind blew from the southeast, and I knew that it would be calm by the next morning, making for ideal conditions for fly fishing for big trout on the Laguna Madre. As I looked up at the sky, I saw a full moon through the trees. Then I saw another orb of light beside the moon. How could this be? I wondered. Was it the sun? Was it another moon? I was puzzled. Then I realized that I was dreaming. As I came to this awareness, the two orbs started moving together. I laid down on the grass and meditated on the light, knowing that what I was perceiving was the eternal Light, not the moon or the sun.

As the two lights joined, they became a larger orb of white light upon which a more brilliant white star was superimposed. The new singular body of light now appeared behind thick clouds, but a tunnel opened up through the clouds that gave me a clear view of the light.

Then, to my surprise, the new combined light pulsated, and a shimmering light came down through the tunnel — all the way to where I was and entered my chest. As it did, I went into ecstasy. Then I heard a man's voice say, "You have done well with this."

Then it was morning in the dream, and it seemed that I had awakened. I was with my sister Marianne and my wife Lynn, who were sitting in the grass close to where I'd received the Light. I told them about the dream, and then realized that it was late in the morning, and that I had to leave for the Laguna Madre. I considered asking if it was okay, but then I realized it was my choice to make. So I said nothing more and left alone.

Like most people who have "big" dreams that foreshadow major life changes, I really didn't get it at first. At the time of the dream, I was still married, and I refused to see the implications of striking out toward my home waters alone. That was not surprising, since I had spent almost 17 years denying the feeling and the fact that my wife and I did not belong together. As for considering an extended retreat to the Laguna Madre, I went there often enough, I reasoned, and a few days on the water each summer was as much as anyone who lived 1800 miles away could hope for.

The good work that the voice referred to was, at first, beyond me. I am prone to depression and self-doubt, and the dream came at a time when I was feeling especially low. Yet upon reflection, I realized that the voice was referring to my growing willingness to follow my heart in the middle years of my life.

In 1994, I left my marriage after meeting someone who seemed, at first, to represent all of the spirit and life that I'd kept at bay for 17 years. Any student of Jungian psychology would have recognized my "bold leap" as a clear indication that I had projected my *anima* — that is, all of my unconscious, unrequited yearning — onto my new partner, and that the relationship would surely collapse under the weight of such expectations. While I would love to go back and redirect my headlong plunge into a new life, I really don't think it could have happened in any other way, for I needed something strong enough to justify leaving a longstanding marriage that was empty at its core and to offset the otherwise intolerable remorse of leaving my only son. Only those who have experienced such things, or who have a prodigious capacity for empathy, will understand how an otherwise good person can be overcome by the power of unrequited needs. In the end, everyone suffered a terrible toll, especially my son Ryan, who thankfully remained in the care of his mother while I floundered in a strange new world.

And so it has taken me almost two years to arrive where I need to be — alone for the first time in 20 years — and my thoughts now turn to that dream in which the celestial lights came together to anoint me with their essence. At a time when almost everything in my life seems broken beyond repair, I ponder the question of what this luminous union could possibly signify. It occurs to me that a more lengthy visit to my home waters might give me a chance to forge a deeper connection with myself, and that fly fishing might serve as the activity through which healing and greater wholeness might be found. As a meditator and a mystic, I have always thought that fly fishing is a complete language of the soul — a literal and symbolic pursuit of sufficient complexity to represent all of the significant facets of psychological and spiritual unfoldment. I have also come to believe that, for many of us, the process of becoming a complete person remains arrested until we can find the right spiritual practice and the appropriate context for its consummation. For some people, an ashram, a retreat center, or a therapeutic relationship might provide the appropriate context. As a lifelong spiritual seeker, all of these contexts have, from time to time, served as estuaries of important spiritual awakenings. But I know now that the Laguna Madre is beckoning me to come and to practice upon her waters, and that it is essential that I respond to this call.

And what is her call to me? The problem that compels me to go to her now is one that afflicts many men who arrive at the middle years of their life feeling unfulfilled. It has been called many disparag-

ing things — and the words still ring in my ears — but such labels are usually applied by frustrated lovers and wives, who see their mates slipping away without really understanding why. On the positive side, this affliction can represent a willingness to keep searching beyond stagnant relationships and conventional forms of fulfillment. Certainly, the problem is much richer and more complex than a disappointed lover's cynicism and fear can ever articulate. But it definitely has its down side.

The problem has deep roots and cannot be merely laid upon a man as a fault of his own creation: Some of us learn at an early age to survive by dissociating from our bodies and true feelings. While effective in the short run, such survival tactics leave us thereafter lacking in our ability to live fully. If we fail to recover this capacity, then we are destined to live half lives, deprived of the fuller measure of passion and spirit that resides in no other place than deeply within us.

I know better than to go and expect anything in particular. I know that the best intentions often fail when it comes to matters of the soul, and that the spirit aligned with nature can make a royal mess of the noblest endeavors. I am reminded of St. Teresa of Avila, who was traveling in her open donkey-driven cart toward the site of a new convent. Already a great success as the reformer of the Carmelites, she was used to finding a way to accomplish what she felt called to do. And yet, on this occasion, she came to a river crossing that was flooded by fresh rains. Angry and frustrated, she asked God, "Why did you do this!?" She heard a voice reply, "This is how I treat my friends." Teresa retorted, "Then perhaps that is why you have so few of them!"

And so, when the warm weather comes, I will head south with my boat and my son, knowing full well that powerful Gulf hurricanes and the often-unyielding winds of deep South Texas may complicate, or even prematurely terminate, my fly fishing quest. If so, then perhaps that is how spirit deigns to treat me now, as a friend. In any case, I know that I will have no regrets for having tried. For I trust that the greater catch I seek lies forever within me, sheltered from the winds and the rains, and responsive to every sincere cast of the heart.

Friday, August 3, 2002, late morning
Arroyo City, Texas

The Pain Subsides

After about four hours, the pain abruptly ceased. While I felt exhausted and weakened, I was relieved that I'd made it through the ordeal.

Unfortunately, neither Tim nor I fished very well. Using small poppers and shrimp patterns, we each caught about a dozen small trout on the Trout Bar. Meanwhile, the big ones eluded us, even though many of them were tailing visibly on the shallow flat. After 10:00, we gave up on the big trout and went in search of redfish. Tim hooked a couple of large reds, but lost them both, and I didn't even hook one. It was looking as though it wouldn't be worth going to the weigh-in or fishing the second day. On the verge of admitting defeat, I suggested we swing into the Mud Hole — a boggy lagoon that's famous for hosting tournament-winning redfish.

I started to feel weaker and a little feverish. I assumed it was from the stingray's toxin, so I just kept on going, thinking that I would soon feel better. I caught two small reds in the Mud Hole, and Tim spotted a sizable tailing trout that he could not reach before it disappeared. Then, looking at my watch, I concluded that our time was up. The tournament was over for us unless we caught a big fish on the way back to the boat.

Facing a 20 mph wind, I trudged through mud and algae toward the boat where Ryan was waiting. Even though my chances of catching a fish were slim to none, I kept some line out just in case.

Then, suddenly, I saw a big red only 15 feet away, head down, cruising slowing through the off-colored water. Since I knew he would see me at any moment, I stepped back so I could load my rod for the short upwind cast, and I dropped the VIP popper on top of the fish's

27

head. Instantly, the fish rose to the fly and hit it so hard that it almost broke my tippet. Within seconds, he had me in my backing.

As I fought the redfish, I checked the time again and realized that landing the fish would mean that we'd have to race to the dock, and then we'd have to drive for 45 minutes to make it to the 5:00 weigh-in. Further, Tim had not caught his redfish, so he was out of the running for the second day of the tournament. Something within me put all of this information together and solved the problem: I simply applied too much pressure on the retreating red. The hook popped free, and when I reeled it in and examined it, I discovered that the hook had bent under the pressure.

I was relieved that the tournament was over.

3

The Return of the Unborn Son

On the road to Texas — mid-June 1997

"Why don't you think of him as the coming one,
who has been at hand since eternity, the future one,
the final fruit of the tree, with us as its leaves?" [5]
Rainier Rilke

I drove into the driveway at Cherry Lane and sat in the darkness. The light in the upstairs window told me that Lynn was already awake and getting Ryan ready for the 1800-mile trip. The smell of pine needles and English boxwood in the moist morning air brought back memories of the years I'd spent there. I recalled planting snow peas in early March, playing Handel sonatas on my baroque recorder on the back porch, and picking scuppernongs from the vines I'd planted. It was a place that appealed to those for whom stability and tradition were prevailing ideals. Over 150 years earlier, Robert E. Lee had ridden his horse down the lane to attend a wedding at our neighbor's pre-Civil War house, and slaves were buried only a few feet beyond our trellis at the edge of the woods. Only the occasional sound of jets overhead broke the spell of timelessness that enveloped Cherry Lane. I had no doubt that Lynn would live out her days in this idyllic place, and that Ryan's childhood home would remain one of the only unchanging things in his world.

---

[5] Rilke, R. M. 2000. *Letters to a Young Poet*. Novato: New World Library.

29

Most of the memories were good ones, and the painful ones were fading. Sometimes I would imagine that leaving had been unnecessary. In my fantasy, I would greet them below the porch steps and tell them that I was home again. I would hold them, and we would weep with relief that everything had been unnecessary, and that our sadness was over. But I never could bring myself to do it, because I knew that, in time, I would find myself, once again, a stranger with a stranger. In the end, the momentary relief would give way to something far more destructive to all of us.

The road trip to South Texas with Ryan was the beginning of the longest stretch of uninterrupted time that we'd had together since I'd left two years before. As we departed from Virginia Beach with my boat in tow, I decided to take the southernmost route to Texas, for I was eager to feel the Gulf moisture in the air and to smell the salt marshes along I-10 through Alabama, Mississippi, and Louisiana. Ryan took his role as my copilot seriously, and he sat with me in the front seat for the first hundred miles or so. Eager to keep me from falling asleep at the wheel, he chattered incessantly and made sure that my coffee cup was kept full. However, fading under the effects of less than five hours of sleep, he soon climbed into the back seat and, under the pretext of tending to his dinosaurs, he fell fast asleep.

I was taking Ryan on a journey into my past, into a way of life that was foreign to him. Having grown up along the Mexican border, I had hunted and fished since before I could remember, and I had been exposed to a harsher side of life than he had known in Virginia Beach. But then again, Ryan had been a warrior since birth, evidencing a personal power and authority that was surprising to me. As he slept, I was able to reflect on some of the experiences in my childhood that bespoke of my own warrior-like zeal.

When I was six, my father gave me my first gun, a Daisy BB gun. The next day, I recall, was a sunny Saturday morning. I asked Dad if I could take my new gun out alone. He said yes with one provision — that I never shoot a mockingbird. I knew that the mockingbird was the state bird of Texas, and that they harassed our cats with impunity. Their incomparable song, however, had not yet impressed itself upon my heart. I was young, perhaps too young to have a gun of my own, and I was feeling the urge that drives and afflicts most young men — to conquer something elusive and wild. Eager to be on my way, I gave my father my solemn promise and went out on my first hunt.

I went across the street into the Pucketts' yard and looked up into the mesquite trees that lined their driveway. Before long, I saw a bird among the leafy branches, but I could not tell what it was. Looking back, I realize that I probably knew what it was, but just didn't want to admit it. I just wanted to shoot my new gun. So I took aim and fired. As fate would have it, the BB went through the bird's heart, and the distinctive black, gray, and white markings of a mockingbird revealed themselves as the bird fell dying to the ground. I was horrified. The immensity of my error paralyzed me at first, but then I knew that somehow I had to tell my father what I had done. So I went back home and found him in the bathroom, shaving. Fearful, I told him what had happened. He remained silent for some time. I awaited my fate, expecting the worst.

Then he said with a stern voice, "Never, never do that again."

I was surprised that he did not punish me. He must have realized that I would pay for my error for the rest of my life.

On the surface, sport fishing may seem to be a trivial predatorial activity, like hunting for birds with a BB gun. But while engaging in this outwardly simple pursuit, the greatness of a man, and the demons that reside within him, may rise up together to form a picture of who he is and what he might eventually become. Fly fishing, in particular — with its elegant complexity — can take this process even further, clarifying the reflection by which we come to know ourselves to an exacting and sometimes frightening degree. Where there is strength, fly fishing can glorify it in a myriad of ways. Where there is weakness, it can be merciless.

The zeal which possessed me to go to the Laguna Madre — in which I presumed to know enough about fly fishing to achieve remarkable things in the span of only a few weeks — was similar to the desire that motivated me on my first hunt. This familiar, impatient yearning was perhaps necessary to rouse me from the comfortable and familiar activities of my life in Virginia and to deliver me to the shores of South Texas in the hottest part of the summer. But by itself, it was insufficient, and a familiar sense of error came early in my quest. Fortunately, when one's zeal dies early enough, something more wondrous may eventually take its place.

When I was 20, only days before my 21st birthday, I had a dream that told about this zeal and its inevitable demise. But it also pointed toward something that would unfold later in my life that could finally fulfill my deepest needs.

In the dream, it was early in the morning. It was still dark, but there was a glow in the eastern sky. I asked my parents to follow me outside, telling them that it was time to reveal my purpose in life. They followed me out onto the driveway where I stopped, raised my arms and began chanting.

As I chanted, part of me stood apart from what was happening and was dumfounded by what I was doing. Lightning began to arch across the sky. I felt a powerful energy awaken within me and course through my body. More lightning appeared overhead until, as I lowered my arms, it struck the ground just a hundred feet away. I raised my arms and repeated this process, again bringing the lightning down from the sky.

My parents, meanwhile, were cowering behind me in fear, not understanding nor accepting this Promethean demonstration. In their fear, they hoisted a lance and threw it into my bacKathy As it entered my body, I was more sad than afraid, for I realized that they had not understood my purpose. I fell to the ground, dying. As they came up and looked down on me with frightened expressions, I said, "I was really your son. But I am the son of the unborn son who is still to come." As I said these words, I had no idea what they meant, but I somehow knew that I was confronting them with a shattering truth — that they had failed, and that a more daunting challenge lay ahead.

My parents in this dream bore no resemblance to my actual parents who, by and large, have supported me throughout my life in my endeavors. In my personal and professional therapeutic work, however, I have come to realize that all parents impose upon their children, intentionally or otherwise, their own limiting beliefs and fears. So, in one sense, the dream could have been dramatizing the subtle influences of my actual parents. But I feel that these "parents" were also aspects of myself who, in not being ready for the fulfillment of the dreamer's vision, simply killed off the subversive element. The dreamer's own zeal accurately reflected my own lofty spiritual aspirations that were, at the young age of 21, still obviously encumbered by unconscious fears and assumptions from the past. I had no idea what lurked within me, nor how it would wreak havoc on my life for many years thereafter. In not understanding what I was up against, I could not begin to fulfill the dreamer's lofty calling to bring the Light into the world. However, the dying dreamer's words gave me hope. In time, perhaps, help would come.

When we come to the waters of life, dreaming of a great catch, we are very much like this dreamer: We have a vision of what is possible, and we are driven to achieve it, but we often fail to understand the process through which we must pass to achieve the goal. This calls to mind the story of Amfortas, also known as the Fisher King. Filled with the passion of youth, the young prince went in search of a way to prove himself, but was totally unaware of the forces that he was up against. In his unthinking zeal, he attacked a Pagan Knight, whose lance left Amfortas with a terrible wound that would not heal. He could only languish in his castle, awaiting the coming of a knight who, in seeing the Grail, would ask the crucial question, "Whom does the Grail serve?" By signifiying his willingness to go beyond his own personal ambition — something Amfortas had been unable to do — the knight would effectively establish himself as the new king and heal the Fisher King's wound.

Amfortas' nephew, Parcifal, was destined to fulfill the Grail quest, but not before succumbing to the same unthinking impulse that afflicted his uncle. Parcifal emerged on the scene as a virtual unknown and impressed everyone by doing what no one else had been able to do: He killed the terrible Red Knight. But when he found his way into the Grail Castle soon afterward, the splendid vision of the Grail rendered him speechless. His youthful passion could not help him in finding his voice and fulfilling the requirements of this great vision — to offer himself in service of the Grail. When he awakened the next morning, the castle had disappeared. He had failed, and he did not know why.

As men, we are possessed by a predatorial impulse that motivates us to take initiative and to confront challenges that range from intellectual puzzles to life-threatening conflicts. This force can take us far beyond the familiar — away from the hearth fires of the family and the community, and over the known horizon into the unexplored regions of our lives. It can get us into a lot of trouble, but its sheer energy can also help us find our way into the Grail Castle. There we discover, as Parcifal did, that the zeal that carries many of us to the threshold of fulfillment has nothing whatsoever to contribute to the next stage in our journey. Whether we seek a trophy fish, the love of our life, or communion with the Divine, we are likely to come up empty-handed the first time we try. Indeed, few of us succeed without first experiencing what only failure can bring us. If we are so fortunate to be granted more than one chance, then we might — as Parcifal did — finally pass the only test that really matters by offering ourselves in service to what we love, rather than seeking to possess it for ourselves.

I'd promised Ryan that we'd stop at a motel with a swimming pool at the end of our first day of travel, but when we checked into the Days Inn in Montgomery at around 9:00 p.m., we were told that the pool was under repair. With characteristic resilience, Ryan said, "That's okay, Dad," and made the best of the situation by playing with his dinosaurs on the bed. Within minutes, he'd fallen asleep in his clothes, dead-tired from our 14-hour drive. Overtired and unable to sleep, I turned off the lights and sat in a chair considering what lay before me, and what I'd left behind.

A few months earlier, I'd met Kathy — a woman with whom I'd felt an immediate deep rapport. In only a matter of weeks, it was clear to her that she and I belonged together, and it made sense to me. I'd never felt so at ease with a woman, but I was not yet ready for another long-term relationship. Despite my hesitancy, her lease came up just before I planned to go away, so we agreed that she would move into the house, at least for the time being. She needed a place to live, and I needed some help with the house and yard during my absence. It was an arrangement of convenience in lieu of making a full commitment.

In the quietness of the hotel room, I realized that all my life I had acquiesced to the pressure of the moment — most often, my own pressure. That's how I'd gotten married in the first place, and I was intent on not repeating that error. I believed that if I consented to this arrangement, Kathy would eventually become another casualty of my untimeliness. I decided then and there that I could not go to Texas with a commitment waiting for me — that, for once in my life, I would make a journey alone. So I called her, while Ryan slept, and told her that she would need to make other plans.

She was shocked. "Do you still want me to come to Texas?" she asked tearfully. We had planned for her to fly down to spend the last week or so with me.

"I'm not sure that makes any sense," I replied honestly. Having nothing further to say, we said goodbye and hung up, and did not talk again for several days.

I had not watched the news before leaving Virginia, and I was surprised to find only after arriving in Montgomery that we were heading toward a hurricane that was brewing just off the coast of New Orleans. Rather than swinging to the north and avoiding the storm, Ryan and I left Montgomery early the next morning and nervously drove south and west one day before the hurricane winds and almost 30 inches of rain came ashore behind us. As I drove through the edge of the storm, Ryan made a fort in the back seat out of pillows and loose clothing, and he emerged anxiously from time to time to hear the latest weather report.

During the trip, I thought many times of my dream about "the son of the unborn son," and considered the likelihood that on one level, the dream had been referring to my son as one aspect of the redemptive force in my life. He and I had both experienced the grief of our parents divorcing. As for myself, my mother had desperately wanted to leave my father for another man when I was only two. I learned later that I responded to her emotional defection by thinking that I was the problem, and becoming insecure in a variety of ways, from throwing tantrums to asking over and over again, "Do you love me?" Later, when I was 16, my mother finally left abruptly to be with her prewar sweetheart. In the days following her departure, I wrote her a letter, pleading for her to come bacKathy Years later, she told me that the letter had devastated her, and that she had written bacKathy But I don't remember ever receiving a response. I gave up after that, and accepted her decision without any further apparent difficulty.

For better or worse, my parents remained entirely silent on the matter of the divorce. Within a year they had both remarried — leaving their six children to deal with their confusion and grief alone. In response to this upheaval, I developed a pattern of radical self-sufficiency, not realizing until many years later that this resourcefulness was, in part, an attempt to avoid depending on others who might end up abandoning me.

Ryan, in contrast, had managed to keep his feelings out in the open, as his mother and I had been available for him to discuss his sadness and his fears. As we drove, and I felt my deep love for my son, I knew that if I could assist him in communicating openly his fears and needs, he and I would, together, embody the redemptive force of the "unborn son." For, as he made his way through grief to understanding and healing, I knew that my own healing would deepen, as well. As a result, we might both reclaim the greater trust and fearlessness that had once been ours.

Our long journey also provided the time to reflect on my soul-level relationship with Ryan and to consider the events surrounding his birth.

Before Ryan was born, I experienced a series of dreams that raised the possibility that an old friend would soon be returning to earthly life. I know that the idea of reincarnation provokes a knee-jerk reaction in a great many people, but this story is not about what I believe, or what I think anyone else should believe: It's about a series of experiences that came unbidden. On the basis of these experiences alone, there is reason to think that I knew Ryan in his previous lifetime as my close friend and mentor who died several years before Ryan was born.

Years before my friend's death, I had a dream in which his father appeared to me. It was one of those dreams that was more real than everyday life, and so it has stayed with me over the years. In it, I was walking through the woods looking for my friend, and I came upon a man whom I recognized as his father. I asked him, "Have you seen your son?" He laughed and replied, "You know how he is — he's always on his way somewhere." The man was seated on the ground, cross-legged, so I sat down with him. He began to look around my head, as if he could see my spiritual aura, and he began to smile and nod, obviously pleased. Then he began talking about something that seemed, at the time, to make no sense at all — his own wife's resistance to becoming my old friend's mother. With an air of great seriousness, he went on to describe how his wife had accepted this immense obligation only at the last moment. I listened respectfully, but I was puzzled throughout.

It was only after my old friend had died several years later that my dream with his father finally began to make sense: It seemed that he was alluding to the same soul's incarnation as my child! Indeed, shortly after his death, my friend began appearing in my dreams, clearly with the intent of returning to earthly life as soon as possible. Since my wife and I had been experiencing difficulty conceiving a child, it didn't make sense that he would, or could, come to us as our child. But his apparent desire to return to life soon was made clear to me through several intense and unforgettable dreams that took place over several years.

In the first dream, he told me something of great importance and urged me to convey this information to some woman, who would then know for a fact that he had "survived" bodily death. However, when I awoke, I could not remember the message, nor recall the identity of the woman. In another, he ended our conversation with a strange handshake, in which some of his fingers were folded bacKathy Later, upon telling this dream to one of his family members, I learned that before my friend's death, he and his son had settled upon the Boy Scout handshake as a "secret clue" that would inform his son that true contact beyond the grave had been made.

In a dream that alluded to this soul's possible incarnation as our child, I was told that he would soon return, but that for some reason, he could not come back to the same family. In the dream, it was clear that I had to greet him at the door if he was to remain. So, when the knock came, I opened the door, and he entered. I was astounded that he was really back, looking very much like himself. I was anxious to make him feel at home. He sat quietly, looking amused while I scurried about, trying to make him feel welcomed. Did he want to read, or to play bridge, I asked? Finally, I just stopped and looked at him, and said, "I'm so glad you're bacKathy"

He said softly, with deep feeling, "I'm glad to be back, Scott."

Then I awoke.

About that time, I also dreamed that I was out in my front yard when I saw my old friend walk up to the gate and enter the yard. I was so happy to see him that I embraced him between two huge loblolly pine trees that stood side by side. As we embraced, I said, "I love you." He said, "I love you, too." As I awoke, I became aware that he was arranging to return to earthly life through the efforts of another young man, whom I did not know.

A few months later, however, my wife and I decided to try to adopt a child, rather than to continue trying to have our own. In spite of the odds against adopting a healthy infant at the time, a friend called within a few weeks to let us know that her daughter knew of an 18-year-old pregnant woman who wished to place her as-yet unborn child up for adoption. Upon their request, we met with the girl and her boyfriend, both of whom wanted to make sure that we would be suitable parents for the child.

It might seem strange that two "irresponsible" teenagers would insist on determining the placement of their child. But unlike most young couples who conceive a child out of wedlock and wish to be free of the burden, they seemed deeply cognizant of the sacred dimensions of this "accident." We surmised from their oblique references to the conception that they had engaged in sexual relations only once — in a wooded area known among the metaphysically minded locals as a special place. Even though the young couple seemed unaware of the mystique surrounding the area, they were obviously convinced that the unintentional pregnancy was somehow overshadowed with great meaning. While still in denial about the importance of carrying the child to term, the pregnant woman scheduled an appointment at an abortion clinic. Ultimately, however, she could not bring herself to follow through.

Other couples that we knew had waited years unsuccessfully to adopt a baby, so it was hard to believe our good fortune when this couple gave their consent for us to adopt the child. The pregnant woman took remarkably good care of herself from thereon, abstaining from alcohol and pursuing a healthy diet. On his part, the young man felt compelled to offer us his support and friendship as the child matured. While this offer seemed ominous at first, we came to realize that the child — as an only child with older parents — would someday find himself without parents and yearn for the connection that a younger father might help to restore.

Soon after the agreement had been reached, my wife and I began having dreams about the familiar soul's return as our child.

In one glorious experience, I dreamed that she and I were outside at night. I looked up and saw a light moving from east to west overhead. I pointed and said, "Look, a shooting star!" But then it stopped and began to fall toward the earth as a brilliant white feather that spun around as it descended. As it neared the ground, it expanded into an orb of white light that hovered about 20 feet off the ground. I knew then that it was the soul of the unborn child. As it approached us and passed directly overhead, it sent out a shaft of white light that entered my chest and overwhelmed me with love. As the experience subsided, I turned to Lynn, and asked, "Did you experience that?!" She looked puzzled, not knowing what I was talking about. Then I awakened.

When I pondered the question of why this soul would want to be with us, I realized that he and I loved each other deeply, and we shared a common pattern that relates to my passion for fly fishing, as well as for my yearning for spiritual fulfillment: He and I were both driven by a fierce intensity and a deep spiritual calling. And we both loved the man Jesus, regardless of what time and religion has done to him. Looking back, I am sure that he knew this better than I did. After meditating and praying regularly for over 50 years, he possessed a profound intuitive knowledge of people and was well known for his spontaneous demonstrations of this capacity. But he also knew better than to tell people what they didn't need to know: He was amazingly discreet about such things. On one occasion, however, I told him that I dreamed about him all the time. He surprised me by saying that he often dreamed about me, too.

"Oh, really?!" I asked. "What were we doing?"

"In one, we were fighting with swords during the Crusades," he replied, like it was the most ordinary thing to be dreaming of events that happened hundreds of years ago.

"Were we fighting each other?" I inquired, worriedly.

"No, we were on the same side," he said with a sad smile, as if to communicate that it was still not a good thing. He would say no more, even though I pressed him for more information.

About that time, I dreamed that I saw him and myself standing among many of our mutual male friends, outfitted in the armor and weaponry of the Middle Ages. Each of the men that I recognized from this lifetime have always expressed a certain competitiveness and warrior-like zeal. We have played bridge, chess, and other competitive games over the years, and we have remained warily on guard in each other's presence. Even so, there is a tenderness and a sadness in each of us, as if somehow we remember returning from pointless battles, broken in spirit and laboring under the pain and suffering that we had inflicted in the name of God.

Whenever I try to dismiss all of this as mere coincidence, I think of the day when Ryan was only three and picked up a biography of my old friend's father that was lying on our coffee table. Pointing to a back cover photo of an aging man holding a fish on a stringer, Ryan asked, "Is this my daddy?"

I am sure that these experiences did not come to persuade me to treat Ryan any differently than I otherwise would, or to think of him more special than others. That would put an unfair burden on him and

constrain my role as his father. No, the experiences — whether literal or symbolic — came to remind me that love survives everything. And someday when I am gone, I hope that this story will assure him of the timeless connection between us.

Someone once asked the late Waldorf educator, Dr. Werner Glas, if he believed in the rebirth of the soul. He said, "No, but I don't believe in the beach either. I walk on the beach." [6]

Every time that I see my old friend in my son's eyes, I walk on that beach, too.

---

[6] Presentation made at the Association for Research and Enlightenment in Virginia Beach, Virginia.

Friday, August 3, 2002, late afternoon
Arroyo City, Texas

My Condition Worsens

It was after 4:00 on Friday afternoon when Tim, Ryan, and I returned to the dock, so it was too late to see a doctor in an outpatient facility. Going to the emergency room seemed unnecessary, and with a high deductible, I'd end up paying hundreds of dollars for only a shot and some pills. So I decided to hold off getting treatment, thinking that the fever was only a reaction to the stingray's toxin.

Kathy was alarmed when she heard that I'd gotten hit by a ray and stubbornly stayed out on the water the whole day. She drew an epson salts bath for me and preached endlessly over my soaking body about taking better care of myself. I was feeling pretty foolish myself as I crawled under the covers and began to shake with fever, but I thought that at least it was all over. Little did I know that the stingray's wound was, by far, the lesser of two evils, and that a battle with a "man of stone" was already underway.

4

The Pagan Knight

Arroyo City, Texas — mid-June 1997

"We have won everything by the lance, and lost everything by the sword." [7]
Sir Gawain's words to King Arthur

I awoke on the first morning of my Laguna Madre retreat to the sight of Ryan tiptoeing into my room in his underwear. My father was also up, having slept in the same room with Ryan. My MacIntosh laptop blinked like a firefly in the darkness, signifying that it was the only thing that was still asleep. Ryan announced that he was so eager to go fishing that he'd been unable to sleep for most of the night. It seemed like an auspicious beginning.

I wanted so much for my father and son to spend time together; for my father was nearing the end of his life, and I wanted Ryan — who lived so far from him — to know and remember his humor and his warmth. My original plan had been to devote myself to bringing them together on the water during the first few days of my retreat. Then, after taking them fishing for a few days, I thought Ryan would want to spend time with his cousins, and I could get a head start on my fly fishing quest. But, ironically, his cousins went out of town just prior to our arrival. When given the option to spend time with his aunts, he told me that he preferred to stay with me on the water. I felt

[7] Johnson, R. A. 1993. *The Fisher King and Handless Maiden.* New York: HarperCollins.

flattered and thrown off balance at the same time. As a result, we were together around the clock for ten straight days. It turned out to be the most frustrating and meaningful time we have ever spent together.

It was a perfect morning. A few anvilheads were dissolving over the Gulf, and there was no rain in sight. The wind was imperceptible, even though we knew that it would begin blowing by late-morning.

We were one of the first boats to head down the Arroyo in the twilight. I had bought live shrimp for Ryan to use, and my father — who was now pretty much confined to the boat due to a problem with vertigo — opted to use bait and to help Ryan with baiting his hoo-Kathy I thought I had juggled everyone's needs admirably and could conceivably look forward to a couple of hours of fishing alone with my fly rod. I had even outfitted us with walkie talkies, so we could stay in touch while I was wading away from the boat.

Just as the dreamer had to die before the "unborn son" could emerge, I discovered over the course of the next three days that I had to put aside my desire to fish alone and take care of those who meant the most to me. This requirement, I later realized, was not merely to free me of guilt so I could have fun later on. It was the first essential stage of a sacred quest, and it had nothing to do with fly fishing or catching trophy trout. It was about paying homage to what really mattered and giving myself fully to the tasKathy But as we left the dock that first morning, I was unaware of all of this. It had been a year since I'd been on my home waters, and I just wanted to fish.

The boat ride down the Arroyo worked its old magic on me. As a child, the ride had taken twice as long, as my dad's aged 25 hp Johnson labored to keep the old plywood boat on plane. Back then, it seemed that we would never reach the bay, and my impatience would mount as images of fighting fish would fuel my fantasies. Although the Honda pushed the Shoal Cat easily at a speed close to 30 mph, my childhood impatience stirred to life again as a flock of brown pelicans slowly passed us by — skimming just inches above the surface of the glassy water. Meanwhile, Dad sat in front of the console with his head bobbing, holding Ryan while the motor lulled both of them into a light sleep.

The first indication that my eagerness was becoming a problem came as we reached the mouth of the Arroyo. In the early morning light, I noticed a nearby boat training a spotlight on us. Looking closely, I could see a boat along the edge of the channel. And further, I could see that a man was waving a white rag — a sure sign of a disabled vessel. Disappointed, but knowing that I was obliged to assist another fisherman in need, I headed toward the boat, unlike two other boats that had passed them by, obviously pretending not to see the disabled vessel in the twilight.

We tied onto the boat and proceeded to tow them three miles back to the public boat launch, losing the best hours of the morning. Ryan, I noticed, was very quiet and sleepy as we proceeded slow-motion back up the Arroyo. I thought that he, like myself, was sorely disappointed that our fishing had been delayed. But, no, he was apparently lost in dreamy thoughts as we pulled the boat to safety. Later he told me how glad he was that we'd rescued the people. "It was like the story of the Good Samaritan, Dad. It felt good to do it." But my disappointment got in the way of feeling good about what we had done.

The morning was rather unsatisfying after that. Ryan constantly wanted to talk to me by way of the walkie talkie, so it was hard to have my hands free to fish. My fly fishing, in turn, evidenced the poor timing that is typical of an angler's first day on the water after months of inactivity. By reacting too quickly, I missed a big redfish that followed my floating deer hair fly and finally struck only 15 feet away. Redfish have an "inferior mouth" — that is, a mouth on the underside of its head — so when it strikes a surface fly, a fly fisherman must pause for a moment to let the fish inhale it deeply enough to set the hooKathy Needless to say, I tried to set the hook before the big fish could eat it, and the fly popped out its mouth. Poisoned by a familiar feeling of irritation, I was aware enough to realize that my attitude was getting in the way. As I turned to go back to the boat, I faced a half-mile walk on a boggy bottom. We had agreed that I would call them when I needed them to come get me, but when I called, they just sat there. When I finally made it back to the boat, I was dead tired and fuming over why they would ignore me.

It turned out that they were sitting and waiting for me, thinking that my silence meant I was catching fish, and wished to be left alone. Not surprisingly, the batteries were dead in the walkie talkies.

My desire to fish had often gotten in the way of more important things. There was a time when I was in high school that Roger and I would take off after school on Friday and drive 90 miles to Falcon Lake, where his family had a fish camp. One Friday, I asked Dad if we could use one of his laundry trucks to drive up to Falcon. Since we often used the truck for hunting and fishing, he gave us his permission, and we were on the road by 5:00. Equipped with our .22 pistols, fly rods, and several quarts of beer, we drove as fast as the old truck would allow. Along the way, however, I noticed that the engine was overheating. We stopped and poured some water in the radiator and quickly resumed our high-speed treKathy Just outside Rio Grande City, the temperature gauge indicated imminent meltdown, so — with considerable irritation — we stopped and opened the hood, only to be greeted by an open fire. Roger cooly poured what was left of his quart of beer over the flames.

"I've seen this before," he asserted confidently. "It's okay now."

We hopped back in the truck and made it to a service station where Roger offered a man $20 if he could make the truck stop overheating. The man did something inconsequential, collected his money, and off we went toward Falcon. As we approached the turnoff for a dirt road that would have taken us the last six miles, the engine began to miss on all but a couple of cylinders. "Whack, whack, whack," it screamed. We cheered it on, hoping that it would not fail us. As the truck's forward progress slowed to a crawl, we opened the doors and stood on the running board, as if we were somehow relieving it of some of its burden. But just as we arrived at the turnoff, the engine died. Strapping our pistols on, and shouldering as much beer and gear as we could carry, we left the truck on the side of the highway and started our six-mile hike over rocky hills and through barbed wire fences to the lakeside camp.

A few days later, Dad had the truck towed 90 miles home to Kenny Barth's auto garage where Kenny pronounced the engine more completely beyond repair than any engine he'd ever seen. I am still amazed, looking back, that Dad did not beat me with a hoe handle and ground me for the rest of my life. I suspect that Kenny — being a fisherman of similar temperament — may have declared the meltdown an act of God and pleaded for clemency.

Of course, when it came to explaining how it all happened, we left out a few of the details.

On the second day of my retreat, Ryan and I went out together. I elected to leave my fly rods behind and help him catch some fish on bait. Again, everything looked promising until I went to load the live shrimp onto the boat and found that they'd all died during the night. Instead of boating the half-mile back up the Arroyo to the bait stand, I reasoned wrongly that Ryan could handle artificial lures well enough to proceed without bait. Then, after reaching the mouth of the Arroyo once again, I realized that I had forgotten the tackle box! Cursing under my breath, I turned the boat around, feigned a cheerful attitude, and retraced the miles back to the cottage. Again we lost the best hours of the day and caught virtually nothing, because Ryan had difficulty casting the lures.

Ryan's continual presence on the water had a way of amplifying the impatience that I was beginning to feel. While our times ashore were full of adventure and good humor, I found that whatever I did to encourage his success on the water somehow failed. I thought I was imagining things at first, but he seemed to want to defeat my every effort. Frustration was welling up within me, and I did not know what to do.

My agitation concerned me. I had come all of this way to embrace fly fishing as a spiritual practice, to attune myself to nature and the spirit within, and to maintain my commitments to my son and my other family members. But I felt caught between these objectives, feeling that I was doing a poor job at everything. I had felt this way many times in my life, so it was not unfamiliar, nor insignificant. That afternoon, I discovered that the first leg of my quest involved confronting a shadowy aspect of my being that lurked behind this familiar dilemma and which threatened the whole enterprise.

While Ryan napped I sat on the dock, trying to settle down. Agitated, and unable to figure out why, I noticed a sheepshead scraping barnacles and limpets off the dock piling with its formidable teeth. Absorbed in its nearsighted quest for an easy meal, the fish ignored me as I peered over the edge of the docKathy Seized by an impulse uninformed by better judgment, I grabbed a rusty, barbless spear that was propped against the boathouse. Then, sneaking up to the edge of the pier, I bent over, aimed, and stabbed at the sheepshead's broad body. The spike passed through its back, but did not hit its vital organs. It struggled and then swam away after sliding off the rusty spike. Suddenly, I was myself again, mortified by my action. I quickly tossed the spear into the grass and went back inside, distancing myself from what I'd just done.

That night, I had a dream that helped me see that something ominous was surfacing in my life.

In the dream, a woman and I were working together to bring a demon to the surface of a dark body of water that was surrounded by a steep wall of concrete. She cast a topwater fly and worked it slowly over the calm water. I cautioned her, saying that the being would soon rise to the fly. As she turned elsewhere to continue her luring tactic, I was suddenly alone. And then, the demon sprang from the water. He climbed up to where I sat on a ledge above the water. He was black as the night and frightening, and his red eyes were glowing and fierce. He grabbed my leg and bit into my right shoe. While I was terrified, I knew that it was important to face him. As he gnawed on my shoe, looking at me defiantly, I said with firmness, "No!" I knew somehow that I had to face him with strength.

I awoke startled, and it took me a while to regain even a feeble sense of well-being. I lay awake for a good while, trying to understand what was going on. If I hadn't dreamt of him before, I would have been totally confused, but I had encountered what Carl Jung termed the "shadow" on many occasions in the dream state. I knew that, in theory at least, he was the personification of my darker, rejected self which needed to be understood and accepted.

It would have been easy to "demonize" the demon in this dream and to fear that something truly evil was afoot. However, the memory of an earlier dream served to remind me that God himself was probably behind this disturbing development. In it, I was in the Holy Land at the time of Christ, and returning from a long journey. Carrying a large gem-studded cross, I turned a corner and came face to face with Jesus and several of his disciples. He wore a stern expression, and said, "I've come to show you what you have built. The only reason I do so, is because your Father wants me to, and because I do it so well."

At that point, Jesus lifted a lance that had a flaming tip. He hurled it at me, and the lance impaled my shirt sleeve against a stucco wall. He repeated this action with a second lance, impaling my other arm against the wall, as well.

The next thing I knew, I was in a gladiator's arena, on the ground. A huge man towered over me, and he told me — with obvious pleasure — that he intended to kill me. Realizing that I was dreaming, I forced myself awake instead of sticking around to see what would happen next.

Without the benefit of depth psychology, I would have been stranded in puzzlement and fear. But with Jung's help, I recognized the gladiator as a symbol of the shadow, whose power was derived from a lifelong suppression of my instinctual self. It had become, apparently, a loose cannon within me, and accounted for such outbreaks of unexamined aggression as my attacking the sheepshead with the rusty spear.

And so, after an initial reaction of fear, I was prepared to regard the demon as something of value that needed my attention. Given his fierceness and apparent hunger, I suspected that he was intent on reclaiming what was taken from him.

In thinking about this division within me, and the disturbing events on the water with Ryan, I thought again of the young prince Amfortas, or the Fisher King. The story of how Amfortas came to be wounded by the Pagan Knight contained for me the truth about the demon that I could suddenly understand and feel through the images of that story.

Amfortas is a young prince who goes into the woods one day looking for a chance to prove himself in combat. By acting impetuously, he becomes afflicted with a wound that will not heal, which is the central problem of the story that must be resolved by the Grail quest.

How Amfortas receives his wound is cloaked in ambiguity. According to one version of the story[8], he grows hungry and comes upon a salmon cooking over an open fire. Seeing no one, he seizes a piece of the fish to eat, only to find that it is much too hot to handle. It burns his hand and his mouth. In another version, the fish's owner returns and shoots an arrow through the thief's testicles, which subsequently cannot be removed. In still a third version, Amfortas is entranced by the love of a woman and encounters a Pagan Knight returning from the Holy Land. Eager to prove himself, Amfortas lowers his lance and charges the stranger. The men fight until Amfortas kills the Pagan Knight — but not before the knight succeeds in castrating the impetuous prince. Regardless of the source of his wound, Amfortas cannot heal, and he suffers continuously. He languishes, awaiting the coming of a peerless knight, whose purity and courage — and willing service to the Grail — will win Amfortas deliverance from his pain. He is thereafter called the Fisher King because fishing is the only activity that temporarily relieves him of his pain.

Why the different versions of the story? On the surface, there were various French and German writers who elaborated on the myth. But there's a deeper reason for ambiguity than mere artistic license. It

---

[8] Johnson, R. A. 1993. *Ibid.*

comes down to the question, "What wounds us in our quest for spirit?" Is it actual contact with the Christ spirit, which is "too hot" for us initially to handle, or is it the retaliation of our instinctual nature, which is offended by our youthful presumption. A final clue indicates that the answer is "both."

It is significant that the Pagan Knight whom Amfortas defeats at such a cost to himself leaves a piece of his lance in the Fisher King's thigh, upon which is written the word "Grail." The genius operating in this great myth never for once lets us forget that the thing that we fear the most about ourselves, and that we endeavor to leave behind — our passionate, instinctual nature — is ever on a divine errand to keep us from seizing the spirit at the expense of the body.

The name "Amfortas" means powerless. Of course, I was he. And the demon was none other than the Pagan Knight within me who refused to let me live without him.

The origin of the shadow reaches back into our early childhood. From the beginning of our lives, our parents — as products of their own families and society's influences — communicate to us about what they find unacceptable in themselves and in others. Hearing and feeling these messages, most of us accommodate our parents by splitting into two beings — a conscious self, who strives to emulate their ideals, and a rejected, "shadow" self who embodies all of the traits abhorrent or threatening to them.

Both my mother and father were outwardly kind and generous, but ultimately — like most of us, to some extent — they deprived themselves of their deeper needs. Despite all of the good they did in raising their children, they denied themselves the passion and the freedom that sought its expression in one way or the other. My father would often dream out loud of the road trips that he would one day take, once his responsibilities were less consuming — but we learned to recognize that distinctive tone of voice. We knew that he would never leave the work and the sense of duty that consumed his life.

My mother, in turn, stayed in a marriage where she did not feel loved, and apparently dreamed about being free one day. I didn't know it until my mother was dying, but she thought she was to blame for the problems in her marriage. This self-blame accounted for how long she stayed married to my father. But, in time, her repressed needs erupted into consciousness, and she left to be with another man.

My father's shadow never acted out in such dramatic ways. It seems to me that he adopted the more acceptable, but equally imprisoning pattern of remaining the good father who projected his shadow upon others who lived "wilder" lives, with whom he tended to express criticism rather than acknowledging his own need to live more passionately. My mother and father adopted the two classic non-solutions to the problem of their repressed selves: The shadow either takes charge and destroys the status quo, as in my mother's case — or it remains imprisoned, as in my father's case. The real solution, as one might expect, lies somewhere in between.

For years, I lived according to my father's path and suppressed the wilder side of my being. By doing so, I could only discover my shadow in dreams and through projection, that is, in another person. In this regard, I grew up with an older boy who conveniently represented the Pagan Knight within me. He lived across the street from us and was my brother's best friend for many years. But unlike Chip and myself, Benny was wild and lived on the edge of social acceptability and the law.

One day, when I was about six, Benny was pushing me around. Since he was 10, he was much bigger and could get away with it. I had just learned how to twist my fingers into a shape that meant nothing to me. But I knew enough to realize that it would get a rise out of Benny. So in defiance of his power, I gave him the finger and immediately paid for it. He promptly threw me to the ground, pinned me down, and spit into both of my eyes to show me how foolish I had been to insult him. It was a humiliating and disgusting moment.

Not surprisingly, I learned to remain on guard around him. Even as we grew older, he would still do disturbing and dangerous things. On one occasion, his fascination with power almost killed me. While I was skin diving on the west coast of Mexico near Puerto Vallarta, Benny went ashore to take a breaKathy As I snorkeled face down, he threw a volcanic rock the size of a brick in my direction "just to see if he could reach me." The rock plunged into the water only a foot from my head.

Benny wasn't always so aggressive and fierce. From time to time through our childhood, he would reveal a softness that remained just as deeply buried in him as my fierceness was buried in me. On one memorable summer day when I was 14, he and I stood side by side fly fishing in a shallow clear lake near the Rio Grande River. Using small poppers and large mayfly imitations, we caught 46 largemouth bass, bluegill, and Rio Grande perch — more fish than we'd ever caught together. When I finally quit fishing and dragged several of the largest bass back to the shore, Benny was waiting with an ice chest full of lake water in the bed of pickup trucKathy

"What are you doing?" I asked.

"We're going to take the fish to that lake next to the cotton gin. We're going to stock that lake with these fish," he said firmly.

"What?! And not keep them?" I could see letting some of them go, but not all of them. In my defense, it was only 1966, and catch and release had not yet become a widely embraced ethic.

"There's hardly any fish in that lake north of town. These fish will spawn there. So come on...let's take them over there."

"But...all of them?" I asked, still not believing that he was serious.

"Yes! " he asserted.

I could see that he wasn't going to change his mind. So we loaded the fish in the water-filled ice chest, and raced across town to the lake. Ten minutes later, we dragged the ice chest down to the water of the new lake and began to release the fish. Benny wore a rare, softer expression, and he seemed at peace with himself that afternoon. He spoke to me of the contribution that we were making, eventually convincing me that we'd done a good thing.

Even though I mistrusted him, Benny and I began to converge toward some as-yet undefined common ground after I left home and went away to college. Once I got some distance from my family and felt my own wilder side coming to the surface, I began to appreciate Benny's raw spirit, and he, too, sought me out more and more as a friend.

One time, he asked me to take a drive with him while I was home from college. We drove southeast along the Rio Grande River until we came upon a high bluff beside the river. The terrain of South Texas is almost universally flat, so this hill of river sand stood strangely alone at the river's edge. We climbed to the top and could see for a long way up and down the river, and into Mexico.

For some reason, Benny wanted to show me this area. He seemed agitated, as though possessed with a new vision of his place in the order of things.

"Isn't this incredible? I feel that I've been here before. Can that be?" Benny was a natural leader, but in that moment, he had only questions.

"It is certainly possible," I answered.

He asked me if I could teach him to meditate. I said, "Sure." Having always been overshadowed by his aggression, I was surprised by his willingness to learn something from me.

A few days later, he and his partner Sharon invited me over to his house for dinner. As we ate, we began to discuss spiritual matters and concepts of the afterlife. But then, in the middle of the dinner, a knock came on the door. Before Sharon and Benny could rise to answer, four men burst though the screen door, carrying drawn handguns and sawed-off shotguns.

"You are under arrest," one of the men announced loudly, "for conspiracy to smuggle narcotics into the United States."

Benny and Sharon did not act very surprised — maybe they knew what was coming, or maybe they were simply in shock — but I was stunned and had no idea what they were talking about. The men ignored me completely, and when they left, they took Benny and Sharon with them without saying as much as a word to me.

It was the last time I saw Benny. I returned to school a few days later, and I kept up with his whereabouts through Roger. A few weeks later, after posting bond, Benny was heading back from Mexico in the wee hours of the morning with Sharon and some friends. Apparently, the driver fell asleep at the wheel. The car left the winding river road and hit a palm tree not far from the sandy bluff above the Rio Grande where Benny had taken me that day. He and Sharon died from their injuries.

In the months that followed, Benny began showing up in my dreams. He appeared deranged, even demonic — intent it seemed on hurting or killing me. I would run from him, scared out of my mind and wondering why he would want to hurt me, his friend. In one dream, I realized it was a dream, and I tried to wake up to escape him. But I couldn't flee in time, and he assaulted me before I could rouse myself from sleep, terrified.

I realized that Benny could really have been there, attacking me as a confused, discarnate soul. That idea did nothing to reassure me. But as a student of Jungian psychology at the time, I also realized that Benny could be the embodiment of my "shadow," that is, those repressed aspects of myself that needed to be owned and legitimized. Along these lines, I speculated that Benny represented my own need for power that I had suppressed under a soft facade of kindness and spirituality — like my father had done.

I also knew that both could be true. He could be "himself" and a part of me. From this perspective, our relationship was continuing to offer us both ways to evolve toward wholeness, even though he was physically dead. Whatever I did in the encounter that represented a breakthrough for me could release him, as well, from his own commensurate soul-level dilemmas.

Before the series of dreams came to a powerful end, I had an opportunity to be "spiritual" in one dream with Benny. He appeared in front of me, holding a knife. He said, devilishly, "I want to show you my new knife."

Suddenly, I realized that I was dreaming! I knew what to do then. At least, I thought I did. I said, "You are only a dream. May the Light of the Christ surround you. Go away." Nothing happened, and Benny crept closer. He was obviously amused by my outwardly "spiritual," evasive tactic. Without wondering how, I obtained a knife of my own, and I began doing battle with him until I eventually disarmed him — an unlikely outcome, since he was much larger and faster than I was in real life. I did not complain.

Then came a culminating dream in the long series of nightmarish encounters. In the dream — the final one with Benny — he had me pinned to the ground, pummeling me with his fists. I knew that he would eventually kill me if I didn't free myself. I managed somehow to free one arm. Instead of hitting him back, however, I reached up and gently stroked his shoulder. Looking back, I don't know why I thought this would do any good. But he stopped hitting me immediately, and he began to cry.

His tears fell into my face, and he said over and over, "I only want to be loved."

Given my last dream with Benny, one might think that the conflict with my shadow would have ended. But after years of spiritual study and dream work, I know that this dialogue will probably never completely end. It will repeat itself in new contexts and with new characters, providing fresh opportunities to forge a deeper bond with various aspects of myself that were orphaned at an early age.

The dream of the demon indicated that the trip to my home waters had set in motion a fresh encounter with my shadow. When I set aside several weeks to fish my home waters, I had to put myself first in a way that neither of my parents had ever done. I was breaking away from their example of self-sacrifice by honoring my own need for adventure and healing. However, by taking Ryan with me, I was putting him at risk of feeling unimportant to me.

As this fact finally dawned upon me, the dream of the demon began to make sense. Given the demon's fierceness and apparent hunger, I suspected that his anger was driven by the experience of abandonment and a need for recognition. I was not so naive as to think that the demon derived his existence from merely one facet of my past, nor existed entirely within me. He was, at first, the orphan created by my parents' own denial of themselves. He was, as well, the castaway created in me by following their example. Then, too, he was the child that felt my mother's longing to leave my father for another man when I was only two. And further, he was the young man who pleaded for her return when she finally left 14 years later.

But the demon lived, as well, in other darkened places. I knew that he embodied the anger and hurt that I had unwittingly awakened in Ryan by divorcing his mother. And, in setting a course to reclaim the fuller self that had been suppressed for so much of my life, I had inadvertently set my son's needs aside and provoked a familiar sense of desertion within him. I had to address the needs of the inner *and* outer child in new ways before I would be truly free, but I wasn't sure how to take care of both of them at the same time. Despite the complexity of our interrelated needs, one reassuring thing became clear to me: The demon within each of us only wanted to be loved.

On the third morning, Ryan and I planned to go out alone again. I figured out how he could fish with a weedless topwater lure alongside me as I fished with my fly rod, so I set him up hoping for the best. We went out before sunrise, this time remembering everything we needed. We headed for an area just north of Green Island and stepped out of the boat in calm, clear water. Wakes announced the presence of cruising redfish and trout, and three nearby fishermen were spending most of their time fighting and landing large reds. I coached Ryan as well as I could manage while casting to surface disturbances. I missed several strikes on a deer hair fly, and then caught a small specKathy Ryan missed two big strikes, too. Everything seemed to go well until Ryan suddenly lost interest and wanted to return to the cottage to play with his dinosaurs. It was ten miles away, and he was too young to remain there alone! I got angry at Ryan, and then at myself for being unable to shake my sense of irritation. Remembering the dream, I realized that the demon was alive and well in me as my stubborn desire to fish alone. Further, the same force was active in Ryan as his need to get his own way. Since I was the nominal adult and had the power to assert my agenda, I persisted one last time in the foolish notion that we were there to fish, and that it was Ryan's problem if he chose not to join me. I stubbornly continued to fish while Ryan sulked aboard the

Shoal Cat, complaining loudly to no one in particular about his desire to be elsewhere. The stalemate turned from bad to worse. Over the course of the next hour, I briefly hooked at least a dozen reds or trout, only managing to land two small reds. One red went into my backing in seconds before the fly came flying back to me. The fish was probably 30 inches long.

Every lost fish deepened my sense of inner turmoil. I couldn't do anything right. Most fishermen — and probably all fly fishermen — will understand it when I say that I felt punished by a force that was much greater than I was. Finally, I turned away from the feeding fish and walked back to the boat. I tried to act cheery, but I was angry again — mostly at myself. To shake my mood, I let Ryan sit in my lap and drive the boat all the way back to the cottage.

During the ride, I contemplated the first three days of my retreat and realized that I had failed in meeting two important goals that I had set for myself — to give my father the experience that he had graciously given me when I was a child, and to pass on to my son an equivalent legacy. In my haste to pursue a fly fisherman's dream, I had failed to take care of my father and my son. As I considered how to do this, I realized that this might mean going all the way back to bait fishing on the dock below the cottage, just as I had done when I was a child. Ryan probably needed this simple pleasure to cement his love for fishing and for the Laguna Madre. Further, my father's age and infirmities required that he, too, return to the simple enjoyment of fishing with bait on the dock at night. For me, it meant letting go.

By the time we arrived back at the cottage, we were both in good spirits once again.

In the Gnostic text known as the Gospel of Thomas[9], Jesus says, "Those who seek should not stop seeking until they find. When they find, they will be disturbed. When they are disturbed, they will marvel, and will reign over all." I've always loved this unorthodox version of the Master's words, because it acknowledges that we must

---

[9]Patterson, S. and Meyer, M. 1994. *The Complete Gospels: Annotated Scholars Version.* Santa Rosa, California: Polebridge.

struggle meaningfully with the truth before we can accept it as our own. From this point of view, salvation is a dynamic process of unfoldment, not a singular event. And so, after a three-day struggle, I firmly acknowledged my error and came up with a simple solution. I called my father and encouraged him to join us for the night — not to accompany me onto the shallows of the Laguna Madre, but to fish with his son and grandson on the dock under the stars, just as we had done 40 years earlier. His enthusiasm was evident, and I knew that in the suspension of my quest for a big fish, I had found something far greater.

As we fished together that night, Dad told me about one of his first experiences fishing under the lights at the Arroyo. It was over 40 years before, and he was fishing with my old fishing mentor, Kenny Barth, and Mr. McAffee, who owned one of the first cottages on the Arroyo. They were having a grand old time when Dad hooked a big trout. As he brought it to the dock, Mr. McAffee tried to scoop up the fish in the dip net, but he only succeeded in getting it half way in the net before it flopped out and came off the hooKathy In an instant, Kenny was in the waist-deep water with the fish in his arms. Having never heard this remarkable story, I realized that Kenny had developed his fish-landing technique years before his encounter with the 42-inch redfish on the flats off Padre Island. He was a man who, obviously, did not hesitate to seize the opportunities that God and nature afforded him, but he was also a man who evidenced the same zeal in helping others.

After fishing that night on the lighted dock, and catching some trout, both Dad and Ryan surprised me by expressing interest in going out in the Laguna Madre the next morning. So we got up early and headed out again to the skinny, clear water north of Green Island. Upon arriving, we found the same fishermen that we'd seen hauling in the fish the day before. We gave them a wide berth and anchored on the north side of them, where we surveyed the water. The gulls soon gathered just to the east of us, announcing the presence of the same school of reds that had been there for several days. It would have been a simple matter to catch several fish by wading a hundred yards or more to the east of the boat, but Dad and Ryan would have been left out of the action. So, I pulled the anchor, got into the water, and pushed the boat toward the diving gulls. When Dad and Ryan could reach the feeding fish, I waded off to the side, and began to cast my popper toward the action.

Using a topwater plug, Dad broke off on a big red. Meanwhile, I began having strike after strike on an orange VIP popper outfitted with a weed guard. The reds were not tailing, but they were making quite a commotion as they cruised just below the surface in about 15 inches of grass-filled water. I cast my fly to the swirls and often had more than one red turn and follow my fly as I stripped it across the calm surface. Some of them struck only when they were within a few feet of me. By that time, I would be on my knees, hoping they would not see me before deciding to take the fly. Others would hear the fly and come at it sideways from several feet away. These sideswipers would come out of the water and take it without slowing down at all.

When I hooked up for the second time — after a strike that Dad and Ryan could hear from the boat — Ryan jumped into the water and sloshed over to join me, leaving his rod behind. He stood beside me, offering encouragement and cheers. As the fish came closer, I handed Ryan my fly rod and stood behind him, coaching him on how to play the fish. We took turns after that, and together we managed to land six reds from 21 to 24 inches long. It was a glorious day.

Looking back over our first two days together, I saw that Ryan had sensed my desire to be off on my own and had reacted to this by sulking and disrupting my fishing. His reaction made perfect sense, for my desire to fish alone must have reminded him of when I'd left three years before.

That night, after our storybook day of fishing on the Laguna Madre, he and I went into Harlingen and had dinner with my sister Judy and her husband Jim. It was a welcome break from tomato soup, canned tuna, and hamburgers, and it was a luxury to sleep on beds with crisp clean sheets.

As we crawled into our side-by-side twin beds that night, the orphan within my son came to the surface of our relationship. After laying quietly for a few minutes, Ryan turned toward me with a serious expression, and asked, "Dad, why did you leave?"

I was taken aback by his question, but relieved that it was coming out. I carefully explained that I had not been happy for a long time, and that his mom and I had never had much in common. I told him that leaving him was the hardest thing I'd ever done, but that living a mile away from him was the best I could do to make sure we could be together as much as we both wanted.

I don't think he heard much of what I said, for it was more important for him to speaKathy He began to cry — a most anguished cry that I thought would never end — and between sobs began talking about his deep sadness and hurt. He said he remembered in detail the day I had left — how his mom had been reading to him, how she had cried, and how he didn't understand. I crawled into bed with him and held him.

"I don't know you, Dad. Sometimes I wish you lived farther away, because knowing you're so close — but not really home — *really* hurts." Then he added, "I don't know if I can ever trust you again."

I did my best to reassure him, but I knew that I could not take his pain away after having caused it. So, I encouraged him to go on and to say whatever he needed to say. He told me that he couldn't talk to his mom about all of this, because whenever he did, she would cry and leave the room. Recognizing his need for me to act stronger than I felt, I held him while he cried and talked. In that painful, sacred space, we began a process that my mother and I had postponed until I was almost 40, and she was dying of pancreatic cancer. Only then had I found the courage to ask the question that Ryan had asked me — a question that had tormented me for nearly 30 years: "How could you leave us?"

After crying for a while, Ryan suddenly sat up in bed and started talking animatedly about his toys. I could see that he'd made it through his grief for now and felt relieved. He said brightly, "Dad, I want to take all of the old toys out of my room, and then bring back only those toys that I want to keep. We can put all the rest away, okay?"

I readily agreed, but I also knew that he was really talking about something else — of letting go of the past and moving on.

A few days later, it came time for Ryan to fly back to Virginia. The night before I put him on the plane, he became sad again as he got into bed.

"I'm going to miss them all so much. Aunt Mernie, Spencer, Granddad, Aunt Susie, Big Ryan...I want to tell them all goodbye." Ryan was allowing himself to feel his sadness in ways that I rarely allowed myself as a child. Again, I crawled into bed and held him.

"Love hurts, doesn't it?" I said.

Ryan nodded, crying freely.

"But it's the best thing we have."

He nodded again, and soon drifted off to sleep.

August 3-4, 2002
Arroyo City, Texas

A Friend Warns Me of a Dread Disease

I spent most of Saturday in bed, with Kathy and Ryan coming in and out of the bedroom to check on me. Tim had headed back to San Antonio, after helping Kathy clean the boat and stow the gear the evening before, but he too expressed his concern with a phone call.

My foot had swollen to the point where I could no longer wear a shoe. I occasionally hobbled to the porch to watch the boats go by and exchange a few pleasantries with several of our guests. I was becoming somewhat alarmed by my condition, but I kept my worries to myself. Kathy had her hands full. Ryan needed her attention, as did our guests, to whom she was serving breakfast and dinner in the main house.

That night I passed in and out of fever, and awoke around 3 a.m. to find my sheets thoroughly soaked with sweat. My foot had swollen even further and was beginning to ooze a bloody, watery fluid from the wound. Alarmed, I covered my foot with two socks and went in search of medication. Finding an opened bottle of Amoxicillin, I took two and went back to bed. When I awakened, I discovered that it was 8:00, which was the latest I'd slept in a long time.

With a cup of coffee in hand, I limped onto the patio and joined three other tournament contestants, who had stayed at the lodge for the weekend. They had used me as a guide on occasion and had stayed with us for the TIFT the year before, so we had become friends.

When I told the men the story of the stingray hit, one of them — Bob Simpson — reminded me that we had sat on the porch a year before during TIFT, and that he had told me about a bacteria that was becoming well known as a serious threat to saltwater anglers. I recalled our discussion about Vibrio vulnificus *exactly a year before.*

65

Since there had been several cases along the Texas coast in the past year, Bob reviewed the information for my benefit.

He recalled that Vibrio *is in the same family as cholera and can become life threatening if not treated immediately. Although many people contract the bacteria by ingesting raw seafood and survive without incident, anyone with a compromised immune system can die within a few hours of infection. Bob went on to recount several horrifying anecdotes of Texas coastal anglers who had died from* Vibrio.

After hearing all of this, I felt fairly confident that I was okay — even if I had contracted the dread bacteria — since I had no reason to suspect that my immune system was compromised. Meanwhile, another regular fly fishing guest who happened to be a pharmacist, overheard our conversation and mentioned that Cipro and Augmentin were the antibiotics known to be effective against the bacteria. In discussing the situation, Kathy and I decided that it was best to be safe, and to obtain some Cipro from Mexico as soon as possible. It was a three-hour round trip to the border town, so she left as soon as our guests had checked out.

Ryan, meanwhile, had remained at home. From time to time, he would peek in the door and, finding me awake, would sit on the edge of the bed playing with the cats.

5

The Seven Sisters

Arroyo City, Texas — early July 1997

"If you will stay close to nature, to its simplicity, to the small things hardly notice-
able, those things can unexpectedly become great and immeasurable." [10]
Rainier Rilke

The day after Ryan flew back to Virginia, I had the opportunity to go out on the bay alone for the first time since I'd arrived in South Texas. Chip was in Mexico, celebrating his 50th birthday, and would return in a few days. Cecil was busy courting Jo, but promised that we'd get together soon. Except for Dad, who planned to join me from time to time, I didn't expect much company for a while.

As I pulled away from the dock and accelerated the Shoal Cat toward the mouth of the Arroyo, three skimmers took up a position about 50 feet in front of the boat. It wasn't the first time that a brown pelican or a group of skimmers had led me down the Arroyo, but I expected them to veer away at any moment, as before. But the skimmers remained poised just ahead and over me, sometimes veering off just slightly before returning to their point position. When the mouth of the Arroyo came into view, I realized that the skimmers had traveled with me for almost five miles, maintaining a constant speed of about 25 miles an hour. I felt honored by their presence.

---

[10] Rilke, R. M. 2000. *Ibid.*

The hardest thing about fly fishing in the Lower Laguna Madre is deciding where to go. While sitting in my Virginia home far away, it was easy to remember the estuary as a short list of landmarks, separated by open water. In my mind, the array of spoil islands, shallow channels, and vast open flats compressed themselves quite neatly around the central landmark of Green Island. But as I entered the bay itself — comprised of over 300 square miles of shallow water — the spaces between these places stretched out and assumed their true proportions. I, in turn, collapsed inwardly, feeling small. I wondered how I ever thought I could locate a large trout in this watery universe — much less catch it on a fly.

Locating trophy speckled trout is at least half the challenge, for their movements are as arcane as any fish to be found. If you fish often enough, you may eventually find yourself standing among dozens of trout from four to eight pounds, and you might think that they gather like this every day. Like Parcifal, who was told that the Grail Castle was simply "down the road and across the bridge," you might think that the big ones will be easy to find next time. But also like Parcifal, who spent half his life trying to find his way back, you may wonder how you could have been so foolish.

As for finding the big ones on a regular basis, I usually search for trophy trout around structure — such as along the banks of the spoil islands, and near the edges of the Intracoastal and other channel drop-offs. Big trout feed and spawn in shallow water, but they like to stay close to deeper water.

During the spring and summer, the biggest trout — heavy with roe and weighing considerably more than they do the rest of the year — tend to gather along the banks of the spoil islands where they spawn about once a week from May until early August. There a stealthy fly fisher can often spot the backs and tails of these fish breaking the surface in ankle- to calf-deep water, and often in the midst of a school of mullet.

Big trout are constantly redefining the best places to fish. From one year to the next, a proven hot spot will shrivel and die for no other reason than the capriciousness of nature, or a subtle logic that no human can ever hope to understand fully. Most of the fly fishers I know find big trout unfathomable and prefer to target redfish because of their ubiquitousness and willingness to take a fly just about any time. But some of us are cursed or blessed by a fascination with difficult things. I never thought of myself that way, but not long ago I had the occasion to run into my high school algebra teacher Mr. Jones. I never hit it off with him, so when I saw him approaching, shaking his finger, I cringed and expected the worst. But instead of reminding me of how I could have done much better in his class, he said, "You!...you are one of two students that I had in 30 years of teaching, who always wanted to solve the most difficult problems first!" I think he meant his statement as a compliment, but I could also hear him saying that I made things more difficult than they needed to be.

"It's the damned difficulty that makes the fun," said James Dodson's mentor St. Cecil when he first introduced Dodson to fly fishing.[11] Of course, catching a lot of big, easy fish rates more highly on the enjoyment scale than most solitary activities, but even as a teenager in Mr. Jones' class, I was already in St. Cecil's camp — that is, more intrigued by the challenge than by the attainment. Perhaps that is why I eventually became entranced by giant speckled trout, because any fly fisher who regularly goes after them will tell you that they are among the most challenging gamefish to be found anywhere. "Tougher than permit!" says Nick Curcione. "Psycho!" exclaims Fred Arbona. But these men also smile when they speak of her. Indeed, if this fish were a disreputable lady, the passion that she would generate in a few would be more than enough to protect her from the contempt of the many.

As I planed along, going in no particular direction, I was reminded of a dream that I'd experienced as a younger man, in which I saw a map of England suspended in space. A young man who was wearing a cape stood with his hands on his hips, looking with apparent confidence toward a rising sun. His face was aglow with the early

---

[11] Dodson, J. *Faithful Travelers*. 1999. New York: Bantam.

morning light. Over his shoulder was a huge X on the map, signifying the place where the Holy Grail could be found. Below the young man, there was an old man holding the Grail up to the young man, but looking at me with a knowing, inviting smile. It was an auspicious dream, but it provided as little practical direction now as it offered then.

As I contemplated my choices, I thought of Marcus Bach, the well-known religious author, whom I had heard speak several years before. He told the story of when he and his wife had the opportunity to relocate either to the West Coast or to the East Coast. All things being equal, they decided to flip a coin. The coin indicated one direction, but they went the other way! I've always liked this story, because when it really comes down to it, I've always preferred my own choices to oracles.

When I reached the Intracoastal, the skimmers continued eastward, but I had this good feeling about going south. So, true to form I gripped the wheel and turned southward.

I headed toward Three Islands, an area six miles from the Arroyo's mouth that consisted of a few true islands covered with Spanish dagger and cactus, and an array of low-lying spoil islands ringed with black mangroves. On the way, I swung out onto the east flats and planed over the glassy surface of the foot-deep water in search of fish. Even in the twilight, I could see wakes retreating in all directions from the boat. Over the years, I'd learned to tell the difference between the anxious erratic flight of a sheepshead, the dogged push of a redfish, and the stately, deliberate wake of a big trout. Of the latter, I could see a few among the other wakes, but I knew better than to stop and try to catch a fish that was already on her way to the next county.

My uncle Moody pointed out the futility of such an approach years before, when I was 13 and hunting deer in a place called the White Swamp in the southwest Alabama woods. Early one morning, he took my cousin Mike and me into the woods, then left us there with instructions about where to meet him that evening.

It was a wet and cold place to be in late November — and it was a bit scary to be left alone there — but Mike and I stayed within sight of each other and kept warm by moving through the woods. The gum thickets were full of deer that day, and by day's end, we had seen dozens of deer. I thought that my uncle would be impressed. But after telling him the news, he just laughed and said, "I'll bet none of them was heading in your direction." Whenever I see fishermen circling the flats looking for fish, I remember the lesson that he imparted that day: At some point, you have to stop and let them come to you.

When I reached the Three Islands area, I anchored the boat on the edge of the Intracoastal. Looking to the southeast, I could see the resort hotels of South Padre Island rising surreally above the horizon, 10 miles away. The sun was just rising, and a gentle wind blew from the south. With the wind and the sun to my back, it was a perfect morning for sight casting, and I felt the eagerness that precedes success and failure alike. Not knowing which it foreshadowed, I strapped on my waist pack, rubbed sunscreen onto my nose and ears, grabbed my fly rod, and stepped off the boat into the cool, knee-deep water.

Since I had anchored close to a spoil island that had partially eroded back into the estuary over the years, the bottom was alternatingly soft and firm, so I could not predict whether my next step would rest securely on a firm bottom or slip a foot deeper through soft mud. It was an ongoing struggle to remain upright. As I looked to the north, I could see that the shallow water between the channel to my right and the spoil islands to my left was at least 100 yards wide all the way back to the mouth of the Arroyo, now invisible in the distance. Every couple hundred yards, there was an opening between the spoil islands, providing a view that stretched out for another mile or so before the shoreline of the Laguna Atascosa National Wildlife Refuge rose above the horizon. I could also see Rattlesnake Island looming in the distance, above the channel spoils to the northwest. The sandy bluff on its eastern side was crowned with Spanish dagger and glowed in the morning sunlight.

I took up a position in the middle of the shallow flat and proceeded to wade to the north. The bottom was covered with a thick growth of shoalgrass mixed with turtlegrass, so I opted to use a weedless VIP popper. Black drum were feeding all around me, and their flickering tails could be seen occasionally breaking the surface in all directions, but I ignored them this time, preferring to use a fly that they despise.

I had gone only 100 feet from the boat when I heard a fish strike the surface explosively back to my right, on the edge of the Intracoastal. It was the unmistakable sound of a big trout feeding.

I turned around, made some false casts off to the side in order not to spook the fish with the shadow of my fly, and then dropped my popper a few feet to one side of the disturbance. I stripped a couple of times, hesitated, and then the water exploded under my fly, leaving a foamy crater in the smooth surface. I stripped, hoping to feel resistance, but no, the trout had missed — and in stripping so hard, I had pulled the fly away. I lifted my line and, without false casting again, placed the fly in the exact spot where she'd hit. Again, the big trout erupted under the fly. But as fate or luck would have it, when I stripped to set the hook, she wasn't there.

One might think that trout have poor eyesight to miss the fly so many times, but we have to remember that trout have rather large mouths with a tender yellow lining that tears easily. Even if the fly does find a purchase in all of that space, it may still tear free as soon as the angler applies pressure. This adds up to a lot of missed strikes, especially if the fly fisher sets the hook on the basis of seeing the fish strike the fly. Believing that the fish has actually become hooked, we may raise our rods and pull the fly away from the fish before she can hit it again.

The best way to fish topwaters effectively eliminates this problem. The key is not reacting to what you see, but responding to feel alone. Larry Haines, a Port Isabel fly shop owner and master fly fisher, actually looks away when he sees a trout bulging behind his popper, so he won't react to the mere sight of the strike.

This delay in setting the hook gives the fish time to strike again — and again, if necessary — until the fly has lodged in its mouth. Only then, after feeling the fish on the line, should the angler raise the rod. It sounds simple, but it takes a lot of practice before an angler can disregard everything he sees and proceed blindly on the basis of feeling alone. When this happens, the angler has successfully tamed his aggression and become fully congruent with the process.

Again, the parallels between the mystic's path and the quest for trophy trout come to mind. When the encounter with the Divine is imminent, the mystic quickly discovers that he must put aside his own agenda and proceed on faith alone. A journal entry in 1974 illustrates the necessity of proceeding blindly into that sacred embrace: "...I look up in the eastern sky and see a large orb of white light many times the size of the moon. I realize that I am dreaming. I yell out in joy knowing it is coming for me. As soon as I do the Light withdraws into the sky as if it is awaiting a more appropriate response on my part. A woman's voice says, 'You have done well reflecting this Light within yourself. But now it must be turned outward.'" I know that I have to turn my eyes away and trust. As I do, the Light descends upon me."

I continued to walk northward, along the edge of the channel, with the gentle breeze to my bacKathy After every couple of steps, I stopped and surveyed the water, knowing that the greatest threat to my success was impatience. I stopped blind casting after a while, knowing how easy it is to "line" a big trout before you ever see her. To remain ready, I held 25 feet of line coiled in my stripping finger and the fly in my hand.

I finally saw what I'd been looking for — the black tip of a tail against some floating shoalgrass about 50 feet away — and then it was gone. It was a trout's tail, and I knew it had to be a big one for its tail to break the surface in 18 inches of water. I stopped and waited, afraid that the slightest movement would telegraph my presence. Then, a wake appeared, heading my way. I knelt low to the water and presented the fly with a sidearm cast toward the approaching wake. My fly landed too far to the left of the fish, and she didn't see it. So, I lifted my fly into the air again, crouched even lower to the water, and casted again, this time out in front of the fish. Before I could strip the fly, she lunged forward and struck with a sucking sound that could have been heard 100 yards away. At the moment I saw her gills flare, I stripped firmly, pulling the fly away from her before she could ingest it. Moments later, the fish saw me and exploded only five feet away. Her retreating wake was punctuated by indignant muddy thrusts, until all signs of her disappeared over the edge of the Intracoastal channel.

Few anglers have ever seen a tailing trout. It's not surprising, really, because big trout often lie very still with only the tips of their tails out of the water. The glossy black triangle looks for all the world like a wet leaf sticking ever so slightly above the surface of the water. A trout tail never exhibits the nervous flicker of a sheepshead tail or the bold waving of a blue-tinged redfish tail, but it will turn slowly like a periscope searching the horizon before slipping beneath the surface.

For years, I never saw trout tailing because I did not think they were there. I fished long and hard for tailing redfish and black drum, but did not know that trout behaved that way, too. Then, one day, Chip told me that he'd gone fishing at Woody's Hole and caught several trout — and that they had been tailing. Needless to say, I was skeptical, so the next time we went out, Chip, Dad, and I boated up to Woody's Hole. We anchored right in the middle of the pass so Dad could fish with bait while we waded out into the shallower water.

However, even before we got into the water, Chip pointed to something that was about 40 yards away, and said, "Look, there's one." I looked, but I couldn't see a thing.

He talked me through it until I could see something out there, but I thought it surely wasn't a fish. Whatever it was, it just sat there like a piece of trash on the water. But then, as I stared at it, it slowly sank like the conning tower of a submarine.

I still found it hard to accept that what I'd just seen was alive. Thomas Kuhn, author of *The Structure of Scientific Revolutions*[12], might have said that I hadn't been able to see tailing trout because my world view did not yet allow for the phenomenon. After Chip showed me what to look for, I saw several more tailing trout and managed to catch a couple of them. We were learning, in Kuhn's words, to "see new and different things when looking with familiar instruments" in places we'd looked before. Since then, tailing trout have become part of my reality. Consequently, I look for them and see them often.

After not catching anything else, I waded back to the Shoal Cat and headed toward the mouth of the Arroyo. On impulse, I pulled over about half way back, and drifted onto the flats between the Intracoastal and the spoil islands, peering into the water with my polarized sunglasses. Trout were all around me! I anchored quickly and slipped into the water. I was able to sight cast to several trout in the 17-20 inch size range, but none of them was interested in my flies. They swam along as if in a daze, having probably fed on the strong outgoing tide earlier that morning. Figuring that I'd arrived too late, I planned to be there early the next morning.

From the beginning of my retreat, I had been planning to sleep overnight on the boat. Even though I envisioned fishing with topwaters in the moonlight, the urge to spend the night on the bay was driven as much by a yearning to commune with Nature and to create a ritual setting for experiencing a meaningful dream. Having located the school

---

12 Kuhn, T. S. 1962. The *Structure of Scientific Revolutions*. Chicago: Chicago University.

of trout, it seemed like a perfect night to spend the night on the boat, even though the moon was in its dark phase. I reasoned that if the school of small trout had been feeding there every morning, then perhaps the big ones would be there at daybreak, as well.

I left the dock just before midnight after tying some flies and packing my overnight gear. The moonless conditions made it necessary to use a Q-beam to find my way back to the place where I'd found the trout earlier that day.

Thirty minutes later, I arrived at the general area, idled onto the flats, and threw the anchor. Turning off the searchlight, I let my eyes adjust to the dark and took in my surroundings. The sky was cloudless except for a thunderstorm brewing over the Gulf. Lightning flashed every few seconds and lit up a massive thunderhead from within. The air was so clear that the storm appeared to be a few miles away, but the lack of thunder and the yellowish tint to the clouds, told me that the storm was far from me.

I sat on the front deck relishing the warm breeze and contemplating the bright sweep of the Milky Way. I meditated for a while, but soon went back to relishing the view: I just couldn't keep my eyes closed for long. Then, remembering that sunrise comes early in mid-July, I decided to lie down and give sleep a fighting chance.

At first I laid my sleeping bag on the raised front deck, but because the Shoal Cat had no railing — and the wind was still blowing pretty hard — it occurred to me that I could easily roll off the rocking boat while sleeping. Although I was anchored in shallow water, I could still conceivably drown wrapped up in my sleeping bag. It was true that when my time came, I preferred to die in my sleep — but not at the age of 45, and not by drowning in two feet of water. So I moved my bag onto the seat cushions in the open cockpit of the boat, and crawled carefully onto them, trying not to scatter them. It seemed like an excellent idea until my weight caused water to pour into the sagging side of the boat through the self-bailing "scuppers." I groaned as the overhanging edges of my bag got soaked. I was tired of moving around, so I laid there, hoping that I could somehow remain mostly dry until morning.

The stars were so beautiful that I stayed awake for some time. From where I lay, I propped my head on an extra cushion and enjoyed the view of my favorite constellation — the Pleiedes, or the Seven Sisters. They shone with unusual clarity, and I could easily count them.

When I was a child, my father would take me outside to look at the stars. Not surprisingly, my first ambition was to become an astronomer. I drew countless diagrams of the planets and stars in pencil and crayon, and fantasized continually about traveling among them some day. Then, when I was about 10, my parents gave me a telescope for Christmas. For some reason, it came without a tripod, but I would lie on the grass and prop my feet up on a chair, and put the telescope on my toes. I could control it by moving my toes around.

Dad remembered most of what he had learned about the constellations during his service in World War II. He has a prodigious memory for things that I tend to forget, like the names of trees and stars and distant relatives. Since we lived in rural South Texas, there were no city lights to speak of, so whenever the sky was clear, the Milky Way and all of the constellations shone with stippled precision above a largely unbroken horizon. Under this natural planetarium, Dad would retell the stories of how he had used the stars to chart courses for his B-29 crew during the War. I remember, in particular, how he would point to one constellation that seemed, for him, to stand out from the others.

"Look," he would say in a hushed voice, "the Seven Sisters!"

I do not remember why he thought that little clump of stars was so special, but my heart always leapt when he pointed to the Pleiades. It seemed to me that they were gathered together with clear intent, as if to communicate wordlessly, *You are not alone.*

I lay there for a while, savoring the view, until I began to drift off to sleep. Passing into the realm between waking and sleeping, I heard something that I had not experienced in months. It was a familiar interior sound — like ocean waves or a rushing wind — and it had often preceded the coming of the Light or the onset of an out-of-body experience. A well-known Tibetan treatise[13] refers to this phenomenon as the "gift waves," and says that it indicates the presence of a spiritual master who is assisting in the development of the recipient.

Regardless of its source, I have always considered it an auspicious event, so I surrendered to it without resistance or fear. A few minutes later, I lost consciousness briefly, but not before I felt myself rocking back and forth on the verge of leaving my body.

The next thing I remembered, I was sitting with a group of men in a wide, open work boat that was about 25 feet long. It was a very bright, cloudless day. I was fully conscious and acutely aware that I had somehow been transported from the Shoal Cat to another place. I wasn't sure that the men could see me, so I remained still and just watched what was going on around me. Where was I? I wondered. I gathered somehow that the men were waiting to go to work inside a building that towered above us in the middle of an ocean. They all wore similar blue-and-white work clothes. I also observed several strange, otherworldly-looking boats passing by, each of which appeared to be exquisitely crafted and personally tailored to its owner's tastes.

Then I realized with a start where I was: *I was on another planet, and the sun above me was another star!* Reeling from this insight, I was suddenly back on the Shoal Cat, looking up at the stars again and listening to the retreating sound of the gift waves.

When I came fully to my senses, I figured that only a few minutes had passed. I lay awake for quite a while, thinking about what had happened.

From one point of view, my experience was remarkable, because — if taken literally — it suggested that I may have visited another star system, light years away. If I calculated the value of the experience in miles, it was certainly the "biggest" experience I'd ever had. But if I measured my trip by how meaningful it was, then it was as ordinary as a trip to the grocery store.

---

[13] Evans-Wentz, W.Y. 1958. *Tibetan Yoga and Secret Doctrines.* New York: Oxford University.

As I lay there, I remembered the Buddhist story about a man who meditated so much that he was finally able to levitate across a river. Excited by his accomplishment, he ran to tell his master. The wise man seemed unimpressed.

"For only a penny," the master said, "you could have taken the ferry."

I had traveled to many places in search of fish. I had lived among fishermen on the west coast of Mexico, hiked to the sources of little-known Blue Ridge streams, and fly fished the holy waters of the Catskills. But except for a few memories that survived from those times, the only thing that endured — and the one attribute that defined me in this world — was a persistent yearning for something that I could not easily name. Just as Parcifal had searched high and low for the Grail Castle, only to find that it was simply "down the road and across the bridge," I had the feeling that by coming back to my home waters, I'd find a simpler solution than levitating across the river or visiting a distant star.

I dozed off and awakened just before daybreaKathy Carefully extricating myself from the wet sleeping bag, I drank some lukewarm coffee from my thermos. And then, as the sun began its advance on the moonless night, I slipped overboard and waded into the twilight toward the sounds of feeding trout breaking the surface of the water.

I Recall a Broken Promise

In between Ryan's visits to the bedroom, I drifted in and out of a feverish sleep. Images and incidents from the past paraded before me, giving rise to the thought that the stingray wound fit into a much larger context of meaning.

Two years earlier on the opening day of the TIFT, my friend and fellow guide Jaime Lopez and I were fishing along the Intracoastal near Woody's Hole, hoping to catch the trophy trout that would clinch the fly fishing division for one of us. Neither of us had ever fished the tournament and were not naturally inclined to do such things, but we had decided at the last minute to give it a shot. Jaime was a hundred yards to the south, fishing from his kayak, while I stood with Woody's Hole to my back, casting a tiny VIP popper over the edge of the Intracoastal channel and stripping it back onto the shallow, clear flat.

As I relished the warmth of the rising sun, a big fish suddenly hit the popper as it approached the edge of the channel. Only minutes into the two-day tournament, I had hooked a trout that could win the fly fishing division for me. I wanted to win badly, since I was still relatively unknown as a guide on the Lower Laguna Madre, but first I had to land the fish. Trout are exceedingly difficult to land without a net. Slippery and energetic, they often get off at your feet, or swim between your legs before breaking the tippet. Thinking of all the deals that I could make with God, or whoever was listening, I came up with an offer that seemed significant enough to ensure a favorable response: I would consent to have a baby with Kathy. Although she had two children by her first marriage, and I had adopted Ryan with my ex-wife, Kathy and I had been talking about having a child of our own and had

81

dreamt of a great soul who wished to be born as our daughter. Kathy had been hoping that I'd agree, but I'd been resisting the idea.

In that moment, I agreed to father a child if I could land the tournament-winning fish. Looking back, it was foolish of me to promise so much for so little. Five minutes later, I landed a five-pound speckled trout that secured my win of the TIFT Fly Division.

After keeping this promise a secret for a few days, I finally told Kathy about it, and so we proceeded with our attempts to conceive a child. But within a couple of weeks, I got cold feet. I was almost 50 after all, and our economic picture was less than rosy, so I changed my mind — on good principle, of course. Kathy was devastated and went into a period of grieving. But I never really looked bacKathy

While I was not so naive as to think of the stingray wound as punishment for a single broken promise, I was aware that it was a fitting consequence for all of the promises that I'd made in the name of love and then revoked over the course of my lifetime.

It was a consequence of life not lived.

6

Letting Go Too Soon

Arroyo City, Texas — early July 1997

"She did seem
Beside me, gathering beauty as she grew,
Like the bright shade of some immortal dream
Which walks, when tempest sleeps,
the wave of life's dark stream." [14]
Shelley

My brother Chip and I headed east down the Arroyo before daybreak, shining the spotlight along the shores in search of deer and coyotes. The drone of the outboard motor limited our conversation to occasional shouts, and except for the Q-beam's erratic probing, there was nothing much to see. This brief period each morning afforded me the opportunity to let my thoughts and feelings range freely in the privacy created by the steady sound and the predawn darkness.

I thought of Ryan, and tears of happiness streamed freely and blew away in the moist morning air. He'd only been gone for a couple of days, and I already missed his company on the water. I was so thankful for how circumstances had thrown us together and forced us to confront the unspoken feelings and pain between us. I knew that the work he and I had done together would bring us even closer in the years ahead.

Meanwhile, it was easy to forget that I was also driving a boat! The blanket of darkness paired with the lack of sleep lulled me into forgetting that danger could lie just ahead. So, with a start, I returned

---

[14] Shelley, P. B. 1999. *The Revolt of Islam.* New York: Bartlesby.com.

to the task at hand and placed the back of the spotlight firmly against my chin, so that I could direct its beam with a mere turn of my head.

As I leaned forward, straining to see what lay before us, I thought of Dad and how he narrowly avoided disaster one day when he forgot what he was doing.

He and his best friend Dr. Cox were heading back up the Arroyo after a successful morning fishing trip. Dr. Cox insisted on cleaning the fish himself, because he found Dad's method inferior to his own. Fishermen cling tenaciously to their own "best" methods, and often argue long and hard over trivial details. However, cleaning fish is a battle most of us would rather lose, so Dad did the smart thing and offered to drive the boat.

While underway, Dr. Cox needed a fillet knife, so he called to Dad to hand him one that was out of his reach. As Dad turned to hand Dr. Cox the knife, he momentarily forgot to look where he was going, and the boat veered suddenly to the right and hit the shore. The boat shot up on the beach and came to a halt, with the motor still running. Shaken but relieved, Dad and Dr. Cox got out and were able to push the boat back into the water and to resume their journey home. They were extremely fortunate, for the boat struck the shore at one of the only spots along the Arroyo where the steep two- to six-foot banks had eroded into a flat beach. If the plywood boat had hit a perpendicular bank at 30 miles an hour, it would have probably turned over, at least — if not broken up on impact.

"We have been very blessed over the years," Dad said to me just recently, while thinking back on this incident and many others like it. With the help of a few minor miracles, Dad has gotten by largely unscathed, but his penchant for remaining out of touch with his experience has been "visited upon his son." Indeed, my own life is strewn with the debris created by oversight and inattention, and the pattern of "checking out" infects every dimension of my life. It is no way to fish, and no way to live for long.

About 30 years ago, I had an experience which underscored my own penchant for becoming distracted by less important things.

Roger and I had driven 80 miles down the Mexican beach to fish in the "third pass," a narrow, swift channel that connected the Laguna Madre's sister bay — the Laguna Madre de Tamaulipas — to the open Gulf. Back then, it was customary for us to pile into our four-wheel-drive Scout, cross the border at Matamoros, drive four hours south on the beach, and then camp on the edge of the pass.

Upon arrival, Roger and I hastily set up our campsite on the beach, and then waded into the pass where we caught several trout and redfish before darKathy After dinner, we laid on our cots in the open air, sipped our Carta Blanca, and enjoyed the view of the stars.

After dozing off and being asleep for a while, I became conscious of rising out of my body, up into the sky. Instead of being on the Mexican beach, however, I found myself high above a wooded area in Virginia Beach. The sun was rising, and the trees were aflame with the early morning light. As I reached out, I discovered that I could fly. But almost immediately, I doubted myself, and I fell to the ground, unhurt. Fully aware that I was out of my body, and in another realm, I picked myself up and got ready to launch myself into the air again. However, at that moment I saw my old friend and mentor — who was still alive at the time — approaching on foot.

I said, "Isn't this great?!"

He smiled patiently, and then said, "I had hoped that you had gotten over your bent for these experiences by now. For He has been here twice already." Shocked by my foolishness and aware that he meant Jesus, I abruptly found myself back on the Mexican beach.

As I entered the next phase of my retreat, I soon discovered that the problem of being distracted and out of touch with what really mattered was still alive and well.

Chip and I came to end of the Arroyo and turned north, heading for Woody's Hole — an opening between the "spoil banks" on the west side of the Intracoastal Waterway.

When dredging of the ICW commenced in the 1940s, the Army Corps of Engineers deposited the "spoil" near the channel's edge, creating a line of spoil banks, or dredge islands, along the waterway. Many of these spoil banks are covered with mesquite trees and prickly pear cactus, providing nesting habitat and cover for aquatic birds. Indeed, wildlife biologists refer to these man-made islands as "rookery" islands in recognition of their importance as nesting grounds.

Most of the spoil was deposited on the west side of the channel, apparently because the engineers anticipated that the prevailing southeast winds would blow the silt back into the channel if it was deposited on the east side. Consequently, there is an almost unbroken line of islands on the west side of the Intracoastal in certain areas, effectively dividing the Lower Laguna in half from north to south. In between the spoil banks, shallow passes permit the tides to flow in and out of the west side. Redfish and large trout often congregate in these passes, feeding opportunistically on the bait that gathers near areas of concentrated tidal flow.

Some of these openings, like Woody's Hole, are deep enough to permit shallow-draft boats to pass through into west side of the bay, even though much of it remains too shallow — except during periods of extremely high tides — to allow most boats to get up "on plane" once they come to a stop. You can get there at high speed by blasting through Woody's Hole or one of the many other passes, but you'd better keep going or you may find yourself beached in ankle-deep water, praying that the tide is coming in.

Before we reached Woody's Hole, Chip and I decided to stop and wade along the "grass line," an area northwest of Green Island. The piled-up, rust-covered dead shoalgrass is so thick there in the summer that the fish can barely swim through it, but they feed up against the grass bank at low tide. At high tide, they venture slowly out into the grass, often tailing as they go. This was where Chip caught a 9.5-pound, 31.5-inch trout two years earlier.

After Chip and I fished unsuccessfully along the grass line for about an hour, I boarded the Shoal Cat alone and boated the half-mile north to Woody's Hole. Chip, meanwhile, elected to stay behind a while longer to fish for the few tailing reds that we had seen. Since we were outfitted with walkie talkies, we knew we could stay in touch and let each other know when and if we located fish.

I anchored on the edge of the channel and waded slowly into position on the southern edge of Woody's Hole, trying to avoid the boggiest areas — and the stingrays. I remembered from past experience that wading the boggy gut itself would wear me out, but I knew that if I fished just to the south of Woody's Hole along the spoil bank, the bottom would be firm. The mullet streamed out of the gut as the tide flowed into the west side, and I thought that the big trout might be there, too, picking off an occasional fingerling mullet.

It was only the third time I'd fished alone since arriving in South Texas, and I found myself wanting to relax and take my time, observing every movement in the water. A large flounder startled me by jumping out of the water every few minutes, and stingrays kept showing up, probably hoping — if rays can hope — that my feet would kick up some choice morsels from the mud. The water was teeming with mullet. As usual, they exploded in panic every time a bird flew by, or whenever I would take a step.

After reading the water for a while, I began casting my spun deer hair fly into water that was about a foot deep. When a trout struck my fly a while later, I wasn't ready. I missed the fish, and it seemed like a sizable one. Frustrated, I began casting again, and within minutes another trout struck explosively. I set the hook, and its open, yellow mouth was the last thing I saw before the tippet snapped.

I changed to a subsurface fly — a green bendbacKathy Over the span of the next two hours, I landed four trout from about 16 to 20 inches long, but nothing larger. I went to get Chip a little while later and told him about the two larger fish I'd missed and lost. I winced as he asked the question that I had already asked myself dozens of times: "So, what's the matter?"

A pattern was emerging. I was losing big fish, and I was breaking off on big fish, but I had not yet landed any redfish or trout over 25 inches long. I had noticed this problem during my days with Ryan, but because he was absorbing my attention, I had put the problem on the back burner.

When I discussed the problem with Cecil, he thought that perhaps I was overreacting initially, then not putting enough pressure on the fish once it was hooked. In other words, I was trying too hard to hook them, then trying too hard not to lose them. He then told me the story of fly fishing for sailfish with renowned fly fisherman Chico Fernandez in Costa Rica. Chico had just hooked and boated a sailfish on a 12-pound tippet after only a 20-minute fight. Cecil and the others were astounded, and they asked him how he did that. Cecil recalled Chico's terse explanation.

"I know what 11 pounds feels like," Chico told them. "You don't know the difference between eight and 15."

While meditating that afternoon, I revisited the problem with the clarity of mind that only deep meditation brings me. I realized that my loss of fish did not have to do with overreacting or being too careful. Those were the symptoms, not the underlying cause. It was hard to admit, but I realized that, on a deep level, I was out of touch with what I was doing. It may seem strange, I suppose, that a fisherman would travel 1800 miles, spend weeks away from work, invest thousands of dollars on a new boat and travel expenses, and still remain somewhat checked out from the experience. But I knew that my tendency to hold back from entering fully into my experiences went far beyond fishing: Like Dad, who turned away from steering the boat to attend to something far less important, this pattern of becoming distracted from my true goal was always present. As the dream with my mentor indicated, if I wanted to commune with the Master — or catch a trophy trout — I had to come down to earth.

One evening in the autumn of 1996 — almost a year before I decided to make a retreat to my home waters — I closed my eyes while grieving the end of a very intense but clearly doomed relationship. Turning to the most peaceful image I could imagine, I envisioned the spacious, calm waters of the Laguna Madre.

As the image of the still waters calmed me, I went on to imagine stalking large trout and redfish with a fly rod. Just as I was imagining hooking a big trout, something began to intrude upon my awareness. As the reverie continued, driven along by some inner force, I saw a boat just within sight, near Green Island. I examined the image, and became aware of a woman aboard the boat who was fly fishing alone. On this first occasion of "seeing" her, I beheld her only from a distance, but I felt her essence deeply and somehow "knew" a great deal about her. In the weeks that followed, she appeared to me whenever I would imagine myself on the bay. Eventually, she spoke to me about my past. Some of our exchanges were so deep and intense that I am still trying to understand them fully.

Who was she? According to Jung, she was my *anima*, or the feminine counterpart of a man who embodies his deep, soulful aspirations toward union and wholeness. Abstractions aside, I have come to think of her as everything that I've ever wanted but could not have, and everything that I've ever had, but could not yet keep.

She came to me most intensely a few weeks later as I was driving Ryan and myself back to Virginia Beach from a fishing weekend in the Blue Ridge Mountains. It was around midnight, and Ryan was fast asleep. My thoughts turned to the woman on the water, and suddenly she was there, with an intensity that I'd not experienced before. With uncompromising fierceness, she summarized her message to me in simple, personal terms: "You always let go of me too soon."

As I drove along on the highway between Richmond and Virginia Beach, she brought back several experiences for me to consider. The memories were similar in theme. While Ryan slept, oblivious to my inner struggle, I relived these experiences with a depth of emotion that I had not felt before. The first memory went back to my early teenage years.

I knew that it was not the way it was supposed to be. My first intimate encounter with a woman should have been with someone I knew and cared for. But I was so introverted during my early adolescence that I could not get to first base with a girl.

In Texas, you could get your driver's license on your fifteenth birthday. Most of us did. And, if you were old enough to drive, you were old enough to cross the border. So there was nothing standing in the way one night when Roger and Mike suggested we go to *la zona*, also known euphemistically as "Boy's Town." For better or worse, it was customary for American boys who lived along the border to cross over into Mexico as soon as they could drive. Our parents tacitly knew about Boy's Town, but most of them looked the other way because somehow it was accepted that, sooner or later, young men growing up in South Texas would do such things.

We went to Las Flores, the Mexican town that was just across the river from my home town of Mercedes. Back then, the muddy unpaved streets were inscribed with such deep ruts that the roads would take you where you wanted to go simply by pointing the car in the right direction.

The brightest part of a border town back then was the zone of prostitution. From a mile away, you could see the glow of glitzy signs that seemed to announce the presence of something more than sex for money. But the persistent odors of raw sewerage and diesel fumes gave testimony to the human struggle behind the thin facade.

Roger and I went into a bar while Mike stayed outside. He was going with a girl back home and expressed his fidelity by buying a bottle of tequila and eating oysters that he purchased from an old lady pushing a wagon on the sidewalKathy He got terribly drunk, burned his mouth on the oysters, and contracted an intestinal bug that plagued him for a whole month — but he remained loyal throughout.

The details of what happened next are less important to recount than the parallels between my own youthful impulsiveness and the behavior of Parcifal who, soon after leaving his mother, encountered a maiden in a tent in the woods. A sumptuous meal had been prepared for her lover, but Parcifal thought it was his. So he devoured it without asking whose it was. He then kissed the woman, took a ring that was also intended for her lover, and left her to deal with the consequences. Parcifal paid for his error eventually, but it took years for him to awaken to his own insensitivity, and to make amends to the young woman whose lover had beaten her upon his return. No such external consequences awaited me, but over the years, I have recalled the experience with ever-increasing discomfort and sadness.

Later, while I sat on a chair putting my muddy boots back on, the young woman—who was not much older than I was—lay there quietly, looking at the ceiling. I could see that she was sad, perhaps crying. Perhaps she was disgusted with herself, and wished to be elsewhere, living a normal life with a man who loved her. Perhaps her remaining innocence had been touched by my own. I will never know, because I left without inquiring.

As I tearfully recalled this experience, the woman on the water gently but firmly repeated: "You always let go too soon."

The second experience that the woman wanted me to recall took place only four years later.

I was drawn to falconry from an early age. When I was 16, I met a guy my own age who raised and trapped hawks and falcons. Forrest encouraged me to trap my first kestrel, the smallest true falcon. Three years later, during my freshman year in college, I trapped a mature, or "haggard," Harris's hawk over the Christmas holidays. She was a beautiful bird that lost her fear of me within days. I took her back to college, and she lived in my apartment with me — perched beside my desk or outside on the second-story balcony. She loved for me to rub her head with a pencil, and she would look on contentedly as I did my school worKathy

As a student, living in an apartment, I could not give the hawk the attention and proper environment that she needed and deserved. But I was young, and I was pleased that I had "manned" this adult bird in only a couple of weeks. And so, in March, I took her back to South Texas for my spring breaKathy There I planned to train her more fully to come to the fist, and then to hunt rabbits with me. Later, I thought, I would set her free.

While at home, I kept her outside on a circular iron perch that stuck in the ground. Her leash was made of a strip of latigo, and I tied it to the perch with a knot that always remained secure — that is, if I remembered to thread the loose end through a loop formed by the knot. For two days, I left her outside at night and spent a good part of each day walking with her and calling her to my fist. I was gradually extending the distance with a longer leash. Everything went beautifully until the third day.

I awoke and went out to feed her. As I approached the perch, I was horrified to see that she was gone! The knot, I realized, must have come loose, for the leather was too strong to breaKathy I knew instantly that I'd forgotten to thread the loose end through the loop!

Frantically, I began running around, looking up into every tree. My thoughts centered on her horrible predicament: She was dragging a four-foot leash that would eventually get caught in a tree somewhere. There she would hang upside down until someone found her or she died. The thought tormented me as I called my friends and asked them to help me locate her.

Later that day, while walking through the neighborhood, I spotted the hawk atop a large ash tree. I tried to call her to the fist, but she was quickly reverting to her wild state. She flew toward the levees south of town, so I ran home and got my hawk trap — a small wire cage with monofilament snares attached to the outside — and a white mouse to lure the raptor to the trap. If I could drop the trap near her, she might come after the mouse and get snared. It was my only hope.

I drove down to the fields south of my house. Eventually, I spotted the hawk sitting on the ground, apparently unsure of what to do next. I knew that she was hungry, because it had been almost 24 hours since I'd fed her. I drove by her and tossed the trap out of the slowly moving car into the open field. She saw it, and began swaying back and forth as hawks do before they attacKathy Then she flew low to the ground, hitting the trap with her feet and turning a somersault as the monofilament loops snared her toes.

I could not believe my good fortune. Ecstatic, I jumped out of the car and foolishly ran out into the field, eager to apprehend the confused hawKathy I only wanted to free her, but I had to get the leash off. Just before I reached her, however, she panicked and broke free.

She flew just above the ground as I ran after her. She climbed into the air as I made one last effort to grab the leash.

It was the last time I saw her. She flew into the nearby woods and disappeared, trailing the leash behind her. I prayed that someone would find her. Maybe someone did — there was a very good chance of it — but I never knew for sure. For years, I could barely stand the thought of what I'd done. She was the last hawk I will ever capture. Like the mockingbird that I killed when I was six, the haggard Harris's hawk will haunt me the rest of my life.

"You always let go too soon," the woman repeated once more. The image of the incomplete knot came to mind to underscore the truth of her words.

The third and last incident that she brought to mind took place in 1992 on the Jackson River, my favorite trout stream in Virginia.

I was fishing below Gathright Dam with my buddy and outdoor writer Bill May from Maryland. We had caught numerous small trout, but had been unsuccessful in catching the larger trout that rose each morning to the black midges. We had tried Griffith's Gnats and other proven surface imitations, but the big fish had ignored our offerings.

During a sandwich break, I observed a fisherman wading into the same area where I'd been fishing earlier. I could tell that he was a master fly fisherman. I learned later that he was Harrison Steeves, a college professor and fly tyer who is widely acknowledged as being one of the best trout fisherman and terrestrial fly innovators in the East. He was nymphing with a short line, and he managed to catch a 17-inch brown and a 15-inch rainbow in the span of a half hour.

I went down to watch him beach the rainbow. He seemed friendly enough for me to ask him what he was using, even though I learned afterward that Harry has a reputation for gruffness in the presence of fools. I guess he thought I wasn't a fool, for he showed me his tiny midge pupae imitation, which I knew would be simple to tie.

That night in the motel, Bill and I tied several of the size 18 midge imitations. We got up early the next morning and went back to the river just below the dam. I waded into the same place where Harry had fished, and in a few minutes I'd caught and released two 15- to 16-inch trout.

My success on the water was not, however, what the woman in my reverie wanted me to remember. She wanted me to consider what happened a few weeks later at the same place.

I was there again casting the tiny midge pupae upstream on my four-weight, seven-and-a-half-foot rod, using a weighted 6x tippet. It wasn't your typical nymphing rod by any means, but I liked the sensitivity of the light rod and the virtual invisibility of the 6x tippet. Suddenly, I saw the largest trout I'd ever seen anywhere rising about 20 feet in front of me. I proceeded to cast the midge pupae to the giant rainbow for over an hour until, apparently, the tiny fly finally swept down the feeding lane between the rocks where the fish had been holding. The next thing I knew, the fish came straight out of the water. She was clearly one of the Lake Moomaw rainbows — known for reaching lengths above 30 inches — and had probably come through the spillway at Gathright. Upon reentry, she sped downstream into my backing and beyond, weaving in and out of three other fishermen, until she finally turned and held in the current. Meanwhile, I eased toward the bank, hoping to play the fish from there. But then, something happened. I was wearing an old, cheap pair of wading boots that had become much too loose for me. Instead of buying myself new ones, I had put it off, thinking I could do without a new pair for a while longer. As I took a step toward the bank, the floppy boot caught on a submerged boulder, and I went down face first into the swift, icy water. Since I was intent on keeping my rod tip up, I couldn't brace myself as I fell. When I came up, my neoprene waders were filling with water, and I was soaked from head to foot. To my surprise, I discovered that the fish was still on, but just at that moment, the fly came loose. I stood there dripping wet, sickened by what had happened — the fly fishing moment of a lifetime spoiled by old cheap boots. Like the loose falconer's knot, the boots came to mind as a symbol of how, once again, I had remained aloof from the full investment in my experience.

"You always let go of me too soon," the woman on the water said one last time.

Many, if not most of us spend a great deal of our lives out of touch with our full experience of life. We pull back during stressful moments and observe our experiences and our feelings from afar — from a more detached, unemotional place. This withdrawal typically upsets the people in our lives who see us retreating from involvement and intimacy. Some of us pull back from our experience out of fear of abandonment, having been deserted at an early age by parents or betrayed by lovers later in life. And some of us are driven by a desire to transcend our bodies and to commune with God. But whether we can trace this dissociation to trauma or to spiritual hunger — or both — most men, in particular, exhibit this tendency to some degree anyway. While this may afford us some advantage over the natural impulses that can make our lives a bit messy, or even dangerous at times, in its extremity it leaves us suspended and checked out, unable to connect with our own experiences. We may make good monks and good soldiers, but we make horrible husbands and lovers.

Those of us who operate chronically from this detached or distracted state of mind, avoid the richness of life around us and remain, for all practical purposes, out of touch with our bodies. Our feelings, our partners, and our fish remain somewhat objectified, apart from us. And so, when we go to set the hook or to make love, we overlook the requirements of the moment, and typically, we remain oblivious to this sad fact except for the feedback that we receive from retreating women and fish. Unlike Parcifal, who eventually offered himself in service to the Grail — that is, willing to relate to his beloved with feeling and reverence — most of us rush forward hoping to seize the prize. When this fails, we withdraw, wounded and out of touch with the heart that gives us life.

Sunday, August 4, 2002, that evening
Arroyo City, Mexico

Kathy Returns from Mexico

Kathy returned near dark, carrying a plastic bag from one of the pharmacies that line the main street of Las Flores, but I was surprised when she produced a carton of Augmentin — not Cipro — from the shopping bag. She quickly explained that she had been ready to purchase the Cipro when the Mexican pharmacist told her that she wouldn't be able to take it across the border. Apparently, on the heels of 9/11 — when supplies of Cipro were inadequate to guard against an anthrax outbreak in the U.S. — the Mexican government was trying to keep its supply for its own citizens.

I was annoyed at Kathy for being unwilling to stash the Cipro in the pockets of her shorts and run the risk of being caught. After all, we both knew that Mexican officials never check U.S. citizens on the way back across the bridge, and U.S. Customs officers rarely if ever check for medications, even though Americans are supposed to have a prescription in hand to justify the possession of prescription drugs. But for better or worse — and usually better — Kathy has always been loathe to break the rules, and this occasion was no exception.

Accepting the situation, I took some Augmentin and went back to bed. And that's where I stayed, except for the most urgent errands. Whenever I stood on my right foot, it felt like a thousand needles were stabbing me. It was also becoming increasingly difficult to walk, so I began depending on Kathy to bring me a container to urinate in, rather than walking the 20 feet to the toilet.

I was aware that Kathy was being uncharacteristically subdued on the matter of whether I should go to the doctor. It was apparent to me that she did not want to admit the possibility that I had a serious problem. On my own behalf, I decided to call the clinic in nearby Rio Hondo early the next day. I didn't tell Kathy, but I was beginning to sense that whatever was going on in my body could, in time, kill me.

97

7

This is Real

Arroyo City, Texas - early July 1997

"For here, there is no place that does not see you. You must change your life" [15]
Rainier Rilke

The memories and insights of letting go too soon came back to me as Chip and I returned to Woody's Hole. I claimed my earlier spot, while he waded behind me to the other side of the spoil banKathy Again, I was fishing alone, but I was discouraged by my failures. Chip caught a nice red, but I caught nothing else. I knew that before I left for home, I needed to come to grips with this pattern of checking out if I wanted to have much of a chance of catching a large trout. Given the intensity of my encounter with the woman on the water and the grief that she brought to the surface, I felt that a process of reconciliation was underway, but clearly, it wasn't far enough along. Otherwise, I'd be landing more fish and not having the kind of dream that came to me that very night.

In the dream, I was wading in the Laguna Madre in a place similar to Woody's Hole. I hoped to see a large flounder that I might catch on my fly rod. As I looked around, I saw what I thought was a flounder. It was huge! But then, I realized that it was a giant stingray. I heard it speak in a woman's voice as I cautiously gave it a wide berth. She was aware of me and angry at me. She held me in contempt for

---

[15] Rilke, R. M. 2000. *Ibid*.

being afraid of her, and I could tell that she intended to attack me if she could. I moved quickly past her and was soon safely out of her reach.

The dream resembled another dream of many years before, in which I met a beautiful woman who was carrying a large red booKathy It was the story of my soul in the earth, she said. I opened it and studied the pictures from long ago and felt the stirring of distant memories. She said, "I have followed you through all of your sojourns. And I am angry!" At that point, she reached for my face and scratched me. I awoke with a start.

Like the demon in my earlier dream, and the woman from this

unsettling dream, the stingray seemed to express an anger borne of my refusal to relate to her. She reminded me of the "Hideous Damsel" who rode her donkey into the castle where Parcifal's fellow knights were celebrating his defeat of the Red Knight: She told Parcifal that he had much more to learn, and she challenged him in front of his peers to embark immediately on the next stage of his journey — the search for the Grail itself. The stingray of my dream was, essentially, challenging me to look at what I'd neglected and not just to celebrate the victories.

I also reflected on my experiences with women and knew that the stingray exhibited the anger I'd heard expressed by my female partners over the years. I'm sure that they were giving voice to the lamentations of my soul, but it was difficult at first to admit my part in it.

One of my earliest memories of withdrawing from life was brought to mind through a final reverie with the woman on the water. This reverie took place on the night that Ryan left for Virginia.

Once again, I imagined fishing in the Laguna Madre, and, like before, the reverie unfolded pleasantly until something took over. Suddenly, I saw myself stepping on a stingray and being stabbed in the right foot by its barbed stinger. I felt intuitively that this wound was the righteous revenge from the past — the retaliation of my own feminine side to my lifelong flight from a full involvement with life. In my reverie, I crawled up onto the front deck of the boat, feeling the pain of the barbed point deep in my foot. Then, my reverie gave way to a childhood memory! I recalled when I was about five years old, playing cowboys and Indians. As we ran around hiding and shooting, I suddenly realized that this was not real. Feeling sad, I abruptly quit playing and walked home, leaving my friends wondering what had happened.

In my reverie I returned to the boat, and the woman on the water appeared. She came aboard, took off her bandana, and wrapped it around my foot as a bandage. The pain became more intense, and I was alarmed, for she seemed insensitive to it. She used one of her flies to fasten the bandana around my leg. She pulled it tight before she fastened it, causing even more pain, and she said with firmness, "This is real!"

Then the reverie was over.

As I waded along, other memories rose to the surface, and everywhere I looked I could see the same pattern of letting go, or giving up too soon, and not facing life with the steadfastness that it required. Several years before, I had enrolled in a weekend improvisational acting workshop and was surprised to see how good I was at it. This is, until I froze up and didn't know what to say. Embarrassed, I walked off the stage. But I didn't get far before the petite woman instructor from

Manhattan was in my face screaming. "Don't you ever do that again. It doesn't matter what you say, but don't ever walk away!"

I thought of Dad again, and I realized that there were many ways that he evidenced this pattern that had become so familiar to me. When my mother had an affair with Dad's best friend when I was two, he cried every night for three months. Then, he realized that he had to put his feelings aside for the sake of his kids and his family. But he admitted to me one evening recently, while he and I sat on his back porch swing, sipping beer, that he never spoke to her about what had happened, and he never asked her why. Sometimes, the most obvious questions are the most frightening to asKathy As I had done in my dream of the stingray, Dad skirted confrontation and went on to live in his own world, hoping that things would get better. By devoting himself to his family and his work, he thought he was still "on the stage," when actually he had walked away from the tougher work of relating to someone who had betrayed him. Mirroring his silence with her own, Mom finally left 14 years later without telling anyone why.

As I considered my own recent failures at fishing in light of my lifelong pattern of dissociation, I suspected that I had to move into my experiences and my feelings more fully; otherwise, painful "corrective" experiences might ensue. I realized, as well, that the reverie presented a realistic picture of what could await me. Indeed, there was a good chance, statistically speaking, that I would actually step on a stingray in the course of wade fishing for 45 consecutive days.

My brother had stepped on a ray near Woody's Hole three years before. He was relatively fortunate, because the barbed stinger had come out, leaving a clean bleeding wound. On the basis of this "good luck," he thought at first he could keep fishing for a while longer, but in a few minutes he was shaking and in severe pain. It wasn't surprising that he couldn't go on, because the stingray's wound is allegedly more painful than a rattlesnake bite. With great difficulty, Chip drove the boat back to the dock and then had to travel 20 miles inland to obtain medical attention. From then on, he gladly wore heavy-duty knee-high leggings that greatly restricted his freedom of movement, but which protected him from another disaster.

A stingray also stung Kenny Barth's wife, Estelle, on her Achilles tendon several years ago, and she fared more poorly than Chip. The wound festered for over a year before it healed. Those who have experienced a stingray's attack agree that it is indescribably painful and often heals very slowly.

Reflecting on what might await me if I "checked out" from my experience, I committed myself to doing whatever I needed to do to avert the necessity of such a corrective measure. But I wasn't sure what form my commitment had to take.

A couple of days later, Dad and I were fishing together out of the Shoal Cat, while Chip and Spencer were fishing in their boat. It was hot and windy, and they had already headed back up the Arroyo toward the cottage. Dad and I lagged behind, hoping to catch just one more fish before calling it a day. Dad is a great fishing partner: He never gives up, even though he may spend several days recovering from his bouts of enthusiasm. He cannot wade very far, nor stand for long in a rocking boat, and he is almost completely blind in one eye. But he always encourages me to stay on the water as long as I want. He told me recently, "I've finally arrived at the point where I enjoy seeing other people catch fish as much as catching fish myself." His enthusiasm for exploring the Laguna Madre with me during his later years is a gift that will remain with me for the rest of my life.

As we approached the mouth of the Arroyo, I asked him if he minded if we stopped for a few minutes at Bird Island, a large spoil bank opposite the entrance to the Arroyo. He readily supported this idea, and as I got out of the boat to wade toward the bird-covered island, he said, "Take your time."

I was grateful for his encouragement, and waded toward Bird Island as he, in turn, began casting around the boat. As I neared the island, I spotted a sizable redfish tail waving in the air only a few feet from the shoreline. Intent on getting there before the tail disappeared, I fixed my eyes on it and forgot to look where I was stepping. The water was so shallow and clear that I never thought to look for stingrays.

Suddenly, I glanced down for no apparent reason, and I saw — just in front of me — a large cinnamon-colored stingray with a tail about two feet long. One more blind step, and I would have felt her stinger in my leg. I stared down at her, wondering what possessed me to look down at that *very* moment. I reasoned that I had been "in my body" sufficiently to respond to my peripheral vision or intuitive perception. In that moment, at least, I benefited from the knowledge that comes from associating fully with my body and with all of its perceptions and feelings. I stepped aside, relieved, and went around the ray. Five minutes later, I was fighting a well-hooked five-pound redfish on my fly rod.

Dad and I had never spoken of living with passion. I suppose that few fathers and sons ever do. The most he ever had to say to me about sex was when he handed me the keys to the car on my first date. With obvious embarrassment, he mumbled almost inaudibly, "Don't get into trouble, son." I knew that he was referring to sex, but I'm really not sure he meant to go that far. He would have been shocked to learn that by the tender age of 15, I'd already been with a prostitute.

I cannot remember ever seeing Dad read a novel, play a game, or express very much outward affection toward my mother or his current wife, Betty. And yet, he worked unceasingly in his business for over 40 years and commanded immense respect and love from his employees and the citizens of my home town. In his later years, the passion in his life has consisted largely of growing tomatoes and roses, visiting his children and grandkids, going to coffee each afternoon with a group of elderly men, and reminiscing fondly about the people that he has known. He is one of the most contented elderly men I have ever known, and I have thoroughly enjoyed his company. But I have always hungered for something more than the source of his contentment.

Coming to terms with my own resistance to living fully has meant deposing the ideal of self-denial that my father has embraced throughout his life and, in turn, unwittingly imposed on everyone around him. But it has not been easy, for what argument can be made against the example of a man who has enjoyed such respect and affection from his family and community? I needed help from beyond myself and, as usual, it came through a dream.

In the dream, my buddy Mike and I were back on the streets of Las Flores. We met a young woman, who may have been a prostitute; it was not clear, but regardless, we struck up a flirtatious conversation and made arrangements to see her later that evening. At that moment, however, I noticed that my father was standing off in the shadows and had overheard our entire conversation. He wore a grim, disapproving looKathy But then, suddenly, there was an explosion of light in the eastern sky. We both turned and looked to see what it was. An orb of white light hovered there momentarily before it approached and passed over us. I turned to look at my father, and his expression had changed. He had forgotten his displeasure with me and was in awe of the Light. Our differences had been overshadowed by something far greater than we were.

Then, there was another explosion of light, and again a brilliant orb appeared to the east. This time, a powerful wind came up and began to blow in the direction of the light. Leaves and dirt swirled around us until I felt myself losing my footing and being drawn toward it. Finally, I left the ground and was carried into the Light.

As I fought my fish, I wanted my dad to share my success. So I cried out, "Dad," and held my rod high above me. Then, I saw him waving to me, obviously delighted. Waving back, I knew that my success was his success and that my passion, his own.

Not long ago during a rare heart-to-heart talk Dad admitted that he's always found me easy to love and that we have always seemed, in so many ways, alike. Ultimately, the Light of a higher love has overshadowed our differences and freed us to be ourselves — as a father and son, and as friends.

Monday, August 5, 2002
Rio Hondo, Texas

I Finally See a Doctor

By Monday morning, my foot was even worse, and the wound was oozing almost constantly. After breakfast, I changed socks, hobbled to the car with Kathy's assistance, and we headed for the Rio Hondo Medical Clinic. Cheryl Dodson, a physician's assistant, examined my foot and announced that she believed the stingray's barb had broken off in my ankle. For some odd reason, I never mentioned Vibrio, assuming that she knew about the bacteria and would have treated me for it if she believed I had contracted it. She wrote me a prescription for an x-ray and encouraged me to keep taking the Augmentin. Knowing that I was virtually uninsured — due to a huge deductible — she kindly agreed to treat me at the clinic at a discount rather than referring me to the hospital. She also gave me an intramuscular injection of a 1,000 mg of Rocephin — to keep whatever infection that might develop out of my bone — and told me to stay off my foot and to keep it elevated.

Ryan was scheduled to leave from Houston the next day and fly back home to Virginia. Being only 13 at the time, airline regulations prevented him from making two plane changes, so we'd planned to drive to the Hill Country for one night at a poolside inn and then take him to Houston the next day in time to make his flight. Knowing that I could no longer help Kathy drive, we scrapped our trip to the Hill Country and made plans for me to ride in the back of the Rodeo with my foot elevated while Kathy drove to Houston and bacKathy Ryan was disappointed, but did not complain.

8

The Crystal Wand

Arroyo City, Texas - late July 1997

*"Even the most exalted states and the most exceptional spiritual accomplishments
are unimportant if we cannot be happy in the most basic and ordinary ways, if we
cannot touch one another and the life we have been given with our hearts."* [16]
Jack Cornfield

It was more than Kathy's absence that made the heart grow
fonder as the weeks went by. If a deeper process had not been at work,
my feelings for her would soon have faded under the light of familiar-
ity. But over time, our bond progressively deepened, revealing dimensions in a relationship that I once only dreamed of.

We had spoken by phone on several occasions since that night
in Montgomery when I told her that I had to make the journey to Texas
without any promises to bind me. Always skirting the issue of our future, we had grown closer as I brought her into each new development
on the water. I felt remorseful for the way that I'd cast her aside, but
there was more to it than a man callously spurning a woman's love: We
both realized our relationship could only be forged in the context of
deep mutual consent. Respecting this need, Kathy neither ran away nor
applied pressure: She waited. She watered the roses, mowed the yard,
and took in the mail while I fly fished almost 1800 miles away. And
throughout, she kept her own needs and interests foremost in mind.

A dream dramatized the necessity of putting my own healing
first before I could be of any use to her or anyone else. In the dream, I

---

[16] Cornfield, J. 1993. *A Path with Heart.* New York: Bantam.

was an Indian named White Cloud. My best friend Eagle Claw had just died and had been laid upon a funeral pyre. It was customary for each member of the community to visit the body and to bless the soul's passage into the spirit world. My wife had grown impatient with me, because I had not fulfilled my duty in this regard. She urged me to visit the body immediately, but I refused, saying that first I had to go into retreat. So I left my home and went into the woods to fast and to pray. On the third day, I returned to the village and went directly to the funeral pyre. I held my hands over Eagle Claw's body, and there was a sudden explosion of energy that took us both into the air. Through a column of wind and fire, we ascended into the sky. Then, later, I was laying on the ground alone. As I watched the sun set in a golden sky, I heard a voice say, "He who heals himself can heal others. And then comes the Light." At that moment, there was another explosion of energy, but this time, it came from within myself. White light surged into my vision, and I soon awakened, vibrating from its effects.

Half way through my retreat, I invited Kathy to join me if she would still come. Tearfully, she said yes. Six years later, in deep meditation, I had a vision of her sitting alone in the same Montgomery hotel room from which I had called her on that night in 1997 to say goodbye. In the vision, I heard her clearly say, "I'm waiting." Her willingness to wait during that pivotal transition in my life was a gift of the highest proportion, and I'm so glad that I had the presence of heart to welcome her back into my life before she had moved on.

According to the Grail legend, when Parcifal was still a child, his mother Heart's Sorrow tries to keep him from being exposed to the allure of knighthood. Having lost her husband and her brother to this manly folly, she wants desperately to protect her son from a senseless and untimely death. But one day, despite her efforts to protect him, Parcifal chances upon five knights in full regalia who are riding through his homeland of Wales. The knights make fun of his coarseness, but Parcifal is so impressed with them that he does not care. He is thereafter consumed by the desire to follow them and will not be counseled by his mother's fears. He finally leaves Wales to pursue his dream of becoming a knight, without evidencing any awareness of his mother's sadness. This insensitivity prevails through several subsequent encounters, including his course treatment of the maiden in the tent whose ring and meal he claimed for himself, leaving her to be beaten by her enraged lover.[17]

Later, after having witnessed the Grail for the first time, Parcifal encounters a woman who is grieving the death of her beheaded lover. When Parcifal tells her that he has visited the castle of the Fisher King and seen the Grail, she reacts with obvious alarm. She knows who he is and why he has failed. She tells him that he has failed because he left his mother without evidencing any remorse whatsoever. The young woman also informs him that his mother—Heart's Sorrow—has since died of a broken heart. Once Parcifal hears this tragic news, he experiences the remorse that accompanies the maturation of a man. And then, as if the revelation of his mother's death isn't enough, Parcifal also encounters on the very same day the woman he ravished in the tent, and whose ring and meal he claimed as his own. He immediately redeems himself by defeating her abusive lover and sending the arrogant man—a symbol of Parcifal's own brutishness—to the King to pledge fealty. Other similar revelations ensue, and it was, as you might imagine, a most painful day for the young knight. But in that pivotal moment in the story, Parcifal gains something that many men never acquire in their pursuit of worldly power — an appreciation for the one who gave him life, a capacity to *feel deeply* for the women whom he had wronged, and a willingness to make amends for his unconscious errors. It is remorse that opens his heart, and it is an open heart that accounts for his eventual success in viewing the Grail for the second time. At the moment the Grail appears to him, he is able to give himself fully to its service, and ask the crucial question, "Whom does the Grail serve?"

---

[17] see p. 90

From the time I was born until I was about seven, I lived across the street from my best friend Roger. He and I spent part of every day together for the first few years of our lives. We were naturally best friends.

Our mothers also had a lot in common. They married hardworking men who became successful, but who ultimately lost touch of their wives' deeper needs. At first, both women accepted their roles as homemakers and mothers and put their families above themselves. But somewhere along the way, they succumbed to the pressures of smoldering dreams. From the little bit that I know, I gather that they did not find what they were looking for. And then, several years later, each of them received treatment for clinical depression. Joyce was the first one to go away to the hospital in Victoria, Texas, where she remained for several weeks. She had always seemed very delicate, but she looked positively frail upon her return from Victoria. Years later, I found out that she'd received electroconvulsive "shock" therapy for her depression. As a psychotherapist, I am aware that ECT is still a treatment of choice for unrelenting depression, but in Joyce's case, the therapy seemed to take more out of her than it gave bacKathy

Mom followed suit a couple of years later and went to the Victoria hospital for about a month. I was pretty young then and had no idea why she went away, nor do I recall her leaving. She was just, suddenly, gone. Dad told us only that she needed some rest, so the experience of her absence was only vaguely unsettling.

After returning home, she went away again before she finally left for good. This time, she headed east to the shores of the Laguna Madre and took a room on the mainland at the Queen Isabella Inn where she stayed for over a month. When I recently asked Dad why she went there, he said "just to get away." When pressed for more details, Dad admitted that he had no idea why she'd left.

Even though I ended up staying 15 miles north of the Queen Isabella Inn during my retreat on the water, there was a time each day when my thoughts would turn southward to the place where my mother must have looked out over the water, waiting for the return of something she'd lost — or, most likely, the arrival of something she'd never known. Whatever she did, I am sure that she did not fish.

When I was 14, I asked Dad if I could buy a .22 pistol. Roger already owned a handgun — a Ruger six-shot revolver. Dad consented without expressing any reservations, probably because by then I'd safely handled rifles and shotguns without supervision.

Once I had obtained Dad's permission to purchase the pistol, Roger and I drove up the highway to Harris Brothers and asked Mr. Harris if we could take a look at his handguns. He was known far and wide for being something of a character, and he looked the part by wearing an old, sweat-stained Stetson and chewing on an unlit stub of a cigar. He was usually pleasant, even jovial, but he was known for his moods, and his temper could flare in an instant. Befitting his image, he kept his shop in total disarray. Unclaimed deer heads, tanned deer skins, and dust-covered boxes of shotgun shells were stacked in every corner.

In response to my request, he reached beneath some of the clutter and came up with a brand-new, Colt six-shot revolver. In the context of such dusty disorder, the new pistol shone like a black pearl. I was sold, so I took my money out and reverently handed it to Mr. Harris. For better or worse, there wasn't any paperwork, or any embarrassing questions. He simply called my dad and asked if it was okay. They exchanged pleasantries, and that was it. A few minutes later, Roger and I rode off with the Colt and a new, sweet-smelling leather holster. For the next several years, I left my rifle at home on most outings, and I hunted with a pistol from the Laguna Madre to the rocky hills around Falcon Lake.

There is something spiritual about a beautiful instrument, whether it is a sword, a flute, or a fly rod. And, while most of these instruments have a distinct maleness, they consist of the raw materials of nature — the mother of us all. Freud considered such instruments symbolic of a singular sexual urge, around which everything revolved and to which everything related. But Freud probably never owned a fine fly rod, because if he had, then he might have reasonably concluded that an erect penis in a man's dream symbolized an unconscious urge to take up fly fishing. He might also have felt a stirring, not unlike a child's love for his mother, as he wielded a wand so perfectly crafted and yet so entirely natural in its composition.

Of course, most of us would agree that while a pistol and a fly rod fit into the same general category — that is, of those instruments used by human predators — a pistol can more easily arouse the worst impulses in a man. And further, it takes a stretch of the imagination to see how a firearm can serve the highest spiritual aspirations. But, after satisfying a man's primitive urges, it may be that a weapon can usher him beyond his urge for power into a more sublime expression of his deeper desires.

In this regard, there is an old story — I think it's Buddhist — about a man who wanted to acquire a magical sword so that he could conquer his enemies. He went to a spiritual master and asked him what he needed to do to obtain this ultimate weapon. The master told him that if he would go to a certain religious shrine in the woods and pray before it unceasingly for a whole month, a snake would crawl out from under the shrine at the end of the month. The master went on to tell him that if he would promptly grab the snake by the tail, it would turn into a magical sword.

Well, of course the man eagerly did what he was told to do. He went to the shrine and prayed unceasingly. And, at the end of the month, a snake slithered out from under the shrine. Following the master's final instructions, the man boldly apprehended it by the tail, and it immediately turned into a magical sword, capable of defeating all of his enemies.

But now that he had the sword, he no longer wished to use it. His feelings had changed, and we are left wondering why.

When I had the dream of the crystal wand and the Light when I was 19 (see Chapter One), I overlooked the obvious similarities between a wand and a fly rod. Though they were distant cousins, the crystal wand transmitted light, held aloft the most delicate spinning circlet of crystal, and could easily be broken. But a couple of years later, another dream made it clear to me that all of these instruments were, beyond their outward differences, capable of serving — or, perhaps, releasing — the highest spirit.

In the dream, God himself appeared to me in the driveway of my childhood home. He did not descend from a cloud as one might expect, nor appear surrounded with light. He drove up in a pickup truck filled with hunting and fishing gear of all descriptions.

Even though God looked like an ordinary man, I had no doubt that he was the Deity: He had a certain unmistakable bearing. He got out of the truck, walked up to me, and said simply, "This is all for you."

I thanked him, but I felt unworthy. So I said, "But I don't deserve it."

He smiled, obviously knowing me well. Then he said, "Will you accept this...for me?"

Struggling inwardly, I repeated, "I...don't know." I walked away and sat down in the grass, unable to give him an answer. Then I awakened.

I have often wondered why I did not jump at the chance of having all of what God intended for me to have. My reticence in the dream puzzled me at first. Perhaps it is because I sensed then, and know now, that accepting such gifts will change our lives forever. For, a soulful gift — whether a fine voice, an artistic eye, or even a champion fly casting style — is a veritable Trojan Horse. Beautiful and beckoning on the outside, it requires a fuller expression of capabilities that we may have been loathe to embrace. When we finally accept the instrument of a deeper calling, we can no longer hide the greater truth of who we are. And then we — not the Benefactor — must face the consequences that follow.

From the very first day on the water to the very end of my quest, I brought my equipment into the cottage each afternoon and examined it with the utmost of care. I laid my nine-foot Sage rod on the double bed and emptied my moist flies onto the table to dry. Then I took inventory of what I had lost and what I needed to replace. The battered flies told the story of the school of trout that I may have stumbled upon, or the ladyfish that had run for 75 yards until it threw the fly with one magnificent leap. I would review the day through the testimonies of these mute witnesses, and I would repair the flies for further use, or retire them if they could not be saved.

If my leader was kinked or knotted, I would discard it and attach a new 12-foot tapered leader. I thoroughly coated the fly line with Glide after soaking the Gunnison reel in fresh water. And then, after supper, I would sit at the vise by the window overlooking the dock and tie whatever I needed for the next day's outing. I kept my equipment close to me until morning, to ensure that it would be there for the morning trip. I would often turn over in the night to find my rod — not Kathy — propped on the pillow beside me. During those lonely nights, I might have considered a trade, but then I might have regretted it by morning, especially if windless conditions prevailed.

I came to appreciate fine equipment and well-designed flies only after settling for much less for most of my adult life. Soon after I graduated from college in 1973 and moved to Virginia, I began to tie my own crude flies and to fish the small, intimate streams of the Blue Ridge mountains, with names like Big Mary's Creek, Irish Creek, and Nettles CreeKathy I ignored the traditional time-tested fly patterns, believing somehow that I could invent designs that would work just as well. Wild brook trout and hatchery rainbows will often take just about whatever you present to them, so I achieved modest success with my own flies. Like Parcifal, who continued to wear a homespun garment beneath the armor that he'd taken from the Red Knight after killing him, I carried an entrenched, unexamined vow of poverty into my adulthood. I proceeded largely without books, mentors, or courses of instruction, because I thought that if I couldn't find my own way, it didn't really count. Of course, I was more stubborn than I was pure, and I could have saved myself years of trial and error if I'd only read some good books and opened myself to the assistance of master fly fishermen. It was true that I could catch bass and uneducated trout fairly well. But I hadn't begun to understand the exasperating selectivity of wild rainbow and brown trout.

As an older man, I can see how my insistence on finding my own way parallels my journey on the spiritual path.

When I was 19, I began to meditate. Within a year, I was meditating up to two hours at a time. As a byproduct of this intense spiritual practice, I began to have frequent out-of-body experiences and to commune with the Light on those occasions when I could fully surrender to it. Such experiences are hard to describe adequately — and probably sound outlandish to one who has not experienced such things — but I came to expect them over the next few years. I felt spiritually alive and close to God, but little did I know, the forces that were stirring to life within me were far more powerful than I was. Like Parcifal, I needed a depth of feeling — a quality of heart — that is usually lacking in a young man. In the East, I might have known that I needed someone to help me understand and integrate the turbulent processes activated by intense spiritual practice. But growing up Protestant had left its imprint on me. Between myself and God, I imagined an open path that I could follow on my own.

One of my favorite stories of such spiritual stubbornness concerns Tibet's "great guru" Milarepa, who lived during the ninth century. Like the myth of Parcifal and the Holy Grail, Milarepa's story [18] expresses a timeless truth about how a man will typically insist on doing it wrong before he learns to do it right.

Milarepa's wealthy father died while he was still a boy, and his greedy aunt and uncle took over the family estate. He eventually left his mother and sister behind and went in search of a way to avenge his family's mistreatment. In his anger, he turned to black magic and, by employing powerful methods of concentration, Milarepa was able to

---

[18] Evans-Wentz, W. Y. (ed). 2000. *Tibet's Great Yogi, Milarepa: A Biography from the Tibetan Being the Jetsun-Kabbum or Biographical History of Jetsun-Milarepa, according to the Late Lama Kazi Dawa-Samdup's English Rendering.* Oxford: Oxford University Press.

bring about the death of his aunt and uncle from a distance. Like Parcifal — who defeated the Red Knight early in his career in a rather primitive, unthinking fashion — Milarepa proved that he, too, could wield power in its most primitive form. Using his prodigious psychic abilities, he made a horse panic while it was tethered to a building where his aunt and uncle were gathered for a wedding celebration. In its effort to free itself, the horse pulled down a critical support timber, which started a chain reaction. Milarepa's aunt and uncle were both fatally injured as the wooden structure collapsed on them. Like Parcifal, Milarepa killed his enemy, but remained, as yet, far from his true calling.

Realizing his mistake, Milarepa went in search of the wise guru, Marpa the Translator, so that he could repent of his error and turn his spiritual and psychic abilities to better use.

By the time I was 30, I had been fly fishing for trout in the East for a few years. My equipment consisted of a cheap seven-weight graphite fly rod, outfitted with a poor-quality reel. I used this rod for everything from 6-inch brookies in streams five feet wide, to largemouth bass in the vast open waters of Back Bay of southeastern Virginia. I possessed only a vague understanding of rod size and line weight, and knew nothing about the relationship between tippet size and fly size. I made up for my ignorance with sheer intensity, and I caught a lot of fish this way.

Even though I could afford better-quality equipment, I resisted the idea of buying it for the longest time. For some reason — and it's hard to admit it now — I persisted in believing that people tend to compensate for their ineptness by spending lots of money on gear. On one occasion, I let my arrogance show while I was fishing with my two friends, Joe and Page, on Mossy Creek — Virginia's premier spring creeKathy As we set out across the pasture to the creek, Page asked, "Scott, what size tippet are you using?"

Aware that this meant a great deal to Page — who did everything with exacting care — I answered flippantly, but honestly, "Four-pound Stren." Any fisherman will know that Stren is a popular brand of spinning reel monofilament, but not something an experienced fly fisher would ever use for tippet material. I knew that my response would pull his chain and convey to him that I didn't need to fool with such finery.

But Page, a retired attorney, put me in my place. With a tight-lipped smile, he replied, "Sounds like reverse snobbery to me." Having almost lost his voice to cancer just two years before, Page cherished every moment of every precious day, and he didn't fool around with inferior equipment. To combat snobbery of the ordinary kind, he allowed himself a vestige from his past — a single cigarette and one drink each day, always before dinner, and preferably seated in a chair that afforded him a good view of the mountains.

As we crossed the cattle fences on the stream that day, Page carried his Winston rod and Orvis reel with obvious care. He considers fine equipment the mark of a gentleman, which he is.

Sometimes, just a few words can turn a person around. From that moment, I became aware of how self-defeating I had been. As I probed deeper into this unexamined attitude, I discovered that beneath my disdain of advice and expensive equipment was an ideal that had been forged in fear. I wanted to prove myself without assistance, and I wanted experience to be my teacher. That seemed noble enough, but it camouflaged an even deeper, underlying anxiety: I wanted to avoid depending on anything that could bend, break, or betray me. Unfortunately, this position often left me stranded, with nothing to assist me but my own fine company. By holding stubbornly to the ideal of self-reliance, I discovered and rediscovered many things that most fly fishermen really don't need to know. I took a circuitous route to the goal, and I owe most of what I discovered to one excellent teacher — failure.

I didn't really understand why I held so fiercely to this position until I met the second significant mentor in my life — Chas Matthews — who laid bare the core conviction behind all of this. He helped me to see that because my mother had turned away from my father and the family, I felt two conflicting impulses: a yearning to reclaim her retreating love, as well as an impulse to withdraw from her and anyone who might hurt me again. And so, my relationship with something as lifeless and innocuous as my fishing equipment became just one more arena in which the desire to connect was constantly undermined by the fear of loss. Since my fear had always won out, I remained aloof from a depth of feeling that would have been there if I'd been able to face the underlying problem.

When we allow ourselves to embrace the finest instruments available to us, something akin to love stirs within us. Whether it is a writer's pen, a fine bamboo rod, or a handgun — shaped from the finest natural materials — they afford us a way to express the fullest measure of our abilities and to approach that elusive ideal of mastery. In the pursuit of excellence, we come to depend on them to serve as the conduit through which our essence becomes known to us and witnessed by others. The rod in our hands becomes, if you will, a midwife who has the power to reveal us or, if broken or lost, to make us disappear again. Consequently, when we allow ourselves to depend on them, we may suffer grievously when they are gone.

Ernest Hemingway must have known this all too well. He carried his prized rods in a foot locker that went with him wherever he traveled. Toward the end of his life, he planned a fishing trip out west, and to be sure that he would have what he needed upon his arrival, he packed his gear in his special box and sent it ahead of him by train. As fate or bad luck would have it, the box was lost in transit. Hemingway was devastated by the disappearance of his finest fishing equipment. Some say that he really never recovered from this loss.

Sometimes the loss of a loved one can also shatter the willingness to embrace a suitable instrument, or to accept our deepest calling. For example, when the Tibetan guru Milarepa was a little older — and was poised to become Marpa the Translator's successor — he consented to be sealed in a cave as the traditional way of completing the final stages of his spiritual practice. Everyone expected Milarepa to surpass his own master's level of attainment during this period of seclusion.

But one morning before sunrise he experienced a sudden overwhelming desire to visit his mother, whom he hadn't seen for many years. Obsessed with the idea that he had to see her, he broke out of the sealed cave and went to ask his master for permission to make the journey back home. Marpa knew that he would never see his most-beloved disciple and successor again, but he gave Milarepa his blessings, regardless. Marpa and his wife took Milarepa into their bed where they held him like their child, and wept together until the sun rose. Then they said their final goodbyes.

Milarepa was on the threshold of completing his spiritual practice and achieving enlightenment when he gave way to the strange impulse to see his mother once again. On the surface, it might seem that he allowed himself to become distracted by mere nostalgia. But, from another perspective, the experience was a necessary step in his own unfoldment. Before he could rise to true mastery, Milarepa had to acknowledge all that he had left behind — his mother and his guilt over having left her. His withdrawal from the world had to be reversed through the awakening of feeling, and who better to call him back to his heart than the one who had given him life?

When he arrived back home, he found that his mother had long since died, and that only a pile of her bones remained on the floor of the abandoned family home. The villagers had become so afraid of Milarepa's reputation that none of them had been willing to enter the house to give her bones proper burial. Milarepa was devastated by his mother's death, and he slept on the floor that night beside her bones. It could have been his greatest moment. But instead of going into his grief and using it to open his heart all the way, he did what many of us do when confronted with such pain: He withdrew. He decided to leave the world behind and to assume the life of a complete renunciate.

The next day he left for the hills and took up residence in an empty cave. Having lost all desire to be in the world and all interest in caring for his physical needs, he subsisted on a diet of nettles and an occasional offering from passing hunters. Hoping to complete his spiritual practice in seclusion, he meditated for long hours every day. But, for some reason, he failed to progress. He probably would have continued in this manner until he died, but his sister and an old friend heard rumors of his whereabouts and eventually found him in a greatly weakened state. He had actually turned a shade of green from eating so much nettles. They convinced him to eat nutritious food and to let them nurse him back to health.

As his vitality increased, his progress in meditation accelerated to the point where he was able to complete his spiritual practice. Through this process, he discovered that good food and good health provide a necessary foundation for advanced spiritual practices. In essence, he was born again into the world through the acceptance of his own body in his spiritual life — which, in so many of the world's great stories of enlightenment, is the unacknowledged key to spiritual completeness.

Both Parcifal and Milarepa initially wielded their weapons at the expense of feeling, remaining oblivious to what they'd left behind. It may seem tragic and unnecessary that the opening of the heart has to be purchased as such a price. While we may hope to spare ourselves and others the pain of our mistakes, an old Catholic prayer suggests that such error and redemption go hand in hand.

O precious sin, that makes necessary
the coming of the Redeemer

Tuesday, August 6, 2002, before dawn
Arroyo City, Texas

I Reflect on My Will to Live

Kathy rose early and prepared to make the drive to Houston. By then, having awakened several times in the middle of the night with me, it was obvious she and Ryan were going to have to make the seven-hour trip alone. I could see that she was struggling to keep up with the emotional and physical demands of taking care of the lodge, Ryan, and me. To top it off, in just two days, she was facing the task of guiding for four straight days in a row — something she had never done, having only obtained her Coast Guard Captain's license just a few months before. In that way we were fortunate. We would have lost nearly two thousand dollars in income and that, too, would have added to the burden of my predicament. However, I know that if she'd had more time to consider my condition, I am sure that she would have insisted on a more aggressive approach to my treatment. But there was no one there to relieve her of her usual duties of preparing meals and coordinating the operation of the lodge. She was constantly on the go.

Oddly enough, these circumstances conspired to put me in charge of my own course of treatment. And while she went to the kitchen to get me my coffee, I realized I had to do something to help her.

I stretched across the bed, grabbed the phone, and called the airline. I explained my predicament, and the Southwest agent agreed to bend the rules pertaining to minor travelers, and book a flight for Ryan from our local airport at Harlingen to Houston. From there, they would make sure he made his connecting flight. Relief washed over Kathy's face when I told her what I had done.

I said goodbye to Ryan a few hours later. I could see that he was worried about me, but I assured him I'd be okay, and that our

123

Christmas visit was just around the corner. As I waved from the porch, I wondered when, and if, I'd see him again.

A few days before the stingray encounter, I awakened from a dream that may have accounted for the uncanny sequence of events and choices that seemed to be taking me closer and closer to death. In it, I was on my knees and weeping. I was saying, over and over, "I have lost so much."

On the surface, the dream made little sense. I have enjoyed considerable privilege in my life and have outwardly suffered little. Indeed, when I compare myself to the countless souls who suffer from hunger, pain, and hopelessness throughout the world, I feel that I have little to complain about. But then again, when we overcome the obstacles to our basic survival — and hunger and violence no longer threaten us — then perhaps we may find that a certain spiritual emptiness and sense of loss remains. Further, beyond the setbacks of our immediate circumstances, there is still the real possibility that as we awaken to the soul's memory, then we may recall significant losses and sources of grief from other times.

Regardless of whether it makes any sense, I felt deeply weary at the time of the stingray's wound. Spending time in bed alone, I discovered to my surprise that I could not muster much enthusiasm for recovering. I kept this realization to myself, fearing that by sharing it with Kathy, I would only send her into panic.

9

A Grief Remembered

Arroyo City, Texas - late July 1997

"The meaning of life is not in quest for one's own power but lies in the service of that which is greater than oneself." [19]
Robert Johnson

When I reached my forties, my attitude toward my body and my equipment began to change. A balding head, a bad knee, and other telltale signs informed me that it was time to "use it or lose it" in several different areas of my life. I also became aware that I'd often hidden behind the limitations of my equipment, whether it had to do with music, angling, or photography. It made a better story to tell myself how much I'd done with so little, than to admit how much more I could have done. I came to this sobering realization on the Laguna Madre about the time when I began fly fishing with Cecil.

I recall that I left the dock that first morning carrying a fairly new but low-quality nine-weight rod equipped with an inexpensive graphite composite reel. I was still trying to get by with inferior equipment. In contrast, Cecil took along two Sage rods — an eight-weight and a nine-weight — outfitted with a Ross Gunnison and a gold Marrayat reel, respectively.

---

[19] Johnson, R. A. 1993. *Ibid.*

Cecil took me to one of his favorite spots near Three Islands. It was a cove surrounded on three sides by spoil banks, uncreatively called "The Honey Hole" by some of the local fishermen. There was a gentle north wind blowing that day in July, pushing the boat along at just the right speed for sight casting. So we opted to stay aboard the boat, rather than wading across the boggy cove.

One of us would stand on the front deck casting blindly until a fish was spotted, while the other would stand alongside helping to spot fish. After making a few casts to cruising or tailing fish, we'd switch off.

The area was full of trout and redfish that morning, so the action was unabated. We repeated the drift several times until we'd stung, spooked, or caught a number of fish. As I recall, we landed several reds and two trout, and made casts to over 20 fish. At one point, after hooking a sizable redfish, I jumped off the boat to fight him in the open water. Suddenly, the spool popped off my cheap reel and fell into the water. Frantically, I scrambled to fetch it and managed to replace it just before the fish made another blistering run for it. I was lucky that day and caught some good fish, but Cecil outfished me. His casts were longer and comparatively effortless. A contractor by training, and an artist on the water, Cecil was patient and confident, and his fine equipment supported his growing expertise.

It was perhaps fitting that Page, the man who had chided me for my "reverse snobbery," also helped me to mend my ways by providing me with my first top-quality rod. He decided he needed a three-piece travel rod, so he offered to sell me his brand-new, two-piece Sage RPL III for a hundred dollars cheaper than the going price. In spite of my lifelong predilection to scrimp on tackle, I couldn't resist such a deal. The Sage RPL III was arguably the best saltwater fly rod made at the time, and it still receives high honors. Unlike some of the other higher-modulus graphite rods that have come along since, the RPL III is user friendly, and so I took to it immediately. I was surprised and humbled by how much a fine rod opened up my horizons as a shallow water fly fisherman.

While a fine instrument may allow us to achieve new heights in the pursuit of our sport, we must do our part, too — and that means rising to a higher level of skill in order to reveal the capabilities inherent in our equipment. This is true regardless of our chosen pursuit. My first Sage treated me kindly, considering how much I'd resisted a top-of-the-line instrument. I suppose I was ready for it. But it was a different story in other areas of my life.

For instance, I had been playing the baroque recorder — the historic precursor of the flute — for about 20 years when the "use it or lose it" philosophy began to dominate my thoughts.

I thought I was pretty good at it, but I'd never played in a group, nor had I employed the assistance of a master teacher. Up to that point, my self-taught, homespun approach to music was about the same as it was to fly fishing: I preferred to do it myself. However, I learned that there was a master player and teacher who would drive from Richmond to Norfolk every other week to teach students. So, with some hesitation and trepidation, I called Dale Taylor and arranged to have my first lesson.

Dale was gracious in his praise of my playing, but he tactfully told me that I'd developed some unfortunate habits in the course of playing for so long without corrective feedbacKathy So he set about to undo the effects of my isolation.

As part of my commitment to delve more deeply into music at that time, I decided to purchase a top-of-the-line, hand-crafted instrument. After doing some research, I settled on an alto recorder made by Rob Gilliam-Turner from Charlottesville, Virginia. A friend told me that Rob had traveled all over Europe studying the surviving examples of original baroque instruments. On his journeys, he had also performed in many of the great halls and cathedrals of Europe in order to research the sound of early instruments in the places where they were often played. So I was confident that one of his recorders would assist me in achieving new levels of skill and performance.

When the instrument arrived, I was moved by its sheer beauty. Carved from cherry wood, it was as smooth as glass. Its mouthpiece featured an extraordinarily wide, curved windway, and the fingering holes were undercut to give it a fuller tone. But, when I finally put it to my lips and blew, I was startled by how badly it sounded. Obviously, something was wrong.

I tried my best to play it, but I could not make it sound right. So I put it away, trying to forget how much I'd spent on it. When Dale came for my next lesson, I reluctantly brought out the instrument to see if he could figure out what was wrong with it. Dale held it and looked at it admiringly for a few moments. Then he put it to his mouth and played it. The sound was broad with rich overtones. He played a virtuoso piece from memory and then handed it back to me.

"This is a different kind of instrument," he said simply. "It will require more from you to play it."

"More of what?" I asked.

"More breath," he said. "You have to learn to fill this instrument if you want to discover what it can do."

After that sobering experience, Dale proceeded to teach me a variety of techniques for supporting the breath and opening my windway. I had to make strange sounds by exhaling violently, and then I would have to hum while I also played the instrument. It seemed pointless at first, but he obviously knew what he was doing. Slowly, the instrument began to reveal its dimensions to me. But it took over two years before I felt comfortable with it.

Around that time, a profound dream reinforced Dale's teaching about the breath, and I could see that learning to breathe more deeply was clearly a metaphor for living more fully in congruence with God's will.

In the dream, Jesus was washing the feet of the disciples, and I was deeply moved when he came to me and knelt to wash my feet. As he washed them, he spoke to me about the need to breathe more deeply.

Perhaps many of us recoil from accepting what God intends us to have, simply because we realize what can happen when we do. People can expect more from us, and others may get jealous of our attainment. And, of course, we can fail in much bigger ways. Regardless, the degree of responsibility increases commensurate to our acceptance of our calling. But if we reject the instruments of our soul's expression, then, by implication, we shy away from the one instrument that presupposes the use of any other — the body, the gift of all gifts.

Ironically, when the call comes to descend from the mountain top — to express ourselves more fully in this world — those of us who have drawn closest to the experience of God's presence may feel that we have the most to give up. And yet, coming down and claiming our body and the instruments of this world is the only conceivable way to complete the journey of the soul.

The story of the fifteenth-century monk Henry Suso[20] often reminds me of my dream of God and the presents that he wanted for me to have. For he, too, had to come into the world to fulfill his spiritual destiny. Ironically, it took a vicious lie to bring Suso to the point of fully accepting his humanity.

Suso had already acquired the reputation of being a great healer and holy man. He spent much of his life in prayer and meditation, often passing into ecstasy for long periods. One day, while he was in prayer, he left his body and encountered a young man who told him that because he had done well in the "lower school," he was being admitted to the "upper school." Suso did not know what this meant, but when the young man asked him if he wished to be admitted to the upper school, Suso gladly assented. The young man then guided the monk upward until they encountered the Master.

To prepare Suso for the upper school, Christ gave him clothing that he would need for his new lessons. He did not give Suso the clothing befitting a monKathy Christ handed him armor and spurs — the acknowledged instruments of a knight. Suso protested, saying that he had not earned his spurs in battle. The Master merely reassured him, "Don't worry, you will."

---

20 Underhill. E. 1970. *Mysticism.* Cleveland: World.

Before Suso returned to his body, Christ commanded him to cease all of his self-administered ordeals. From now on, he was told, the Master would administer the tests. When Suso asked what that would be, the Master said, "If I told you, you would not want to proceed."

Unsure of what all of this meant, Suso returned to his body and thereafter waited patiently for something to happen. A few weeks later, the lesson commenced when a woman in the community accused him of being the father of her baby! Suso was understandably devastated, unable to comprehend why someone would do such a thing.

Suso's holiness could not protect him from the woman's lie, and the rumors that followed. His reputation plummeted, and his faith was deeply shaken. In the midst of all this turmoil, a woman in the community approached him secretly and told him that she was in a position to eliminate his problem — by having the baby killed. Suso was horrified by her offer, but asked her to bring the child to him, nonetheless. He wanted to see the child who was at the center of all of the controversy and make sure that it would not be harmed.

Thinking that Suso merely wanted to kill the child himself, the woman eagerly brought the baby to him. As Suso held the baby, he was overwhelmed by love. And, in that moment, he decided to support the child with the little bit of money that he had.

Of course, his heartfelt gesture merely confirmed the mother's story in the eyes of the community, but it had a wonderful effect on him. His courageous act began to dissolve his sense of victimization. In time, he even reached the point where the lies and rumors no longer concerned him.

Even though Suso had not conceived the child, something had been awakened in him through the agency of a lie — the courage to do what was right regardless of the consequences to his own reputation. Clearly, the Master wanted him to live fully as a man — here — as a way to glorify the spirit fully at its farthest outpost.

I feel sure that this is the most difficult lesson that many of us have to face. For instance, when I was about 24, I had a dream in which I first saw Jesus face-to-face. At the time, I was contemplating retreating from my chosen career path as a counselor and speaker. As I stood before him, Jesus conveyed an overpowering love and authority. I knew he loved me just as I was, but he looked stern nonetheless. After a few moments of silence, he asked me a question. "Are you ready to leave the earth yet?"

I was stunned by the implications of this question, and I said, "No."

Then he said, "Then go out and do what you know to do."

Go out. Use what has been given. Claim the gifts that you would gladly disavow out of fear or in the name of spirituality. Retreating from the world may seem to work at first. But, ultimately, it is a path without heart.

We have a choice. We can accept the gifts that spirit intends for us to use. Or, we can drift away into one of the many forms of abdication available to us. Embracing the instruments of our calling is not without danger. For we can easily become overwhelmed by the burdens that accompany the gifts, and we can do harm as well as good with the power that such instruments confer.

"We have won everything by the lance, and we have lost everything by the sword." Gawain's words to King Arthur toward the end of one of the Grail accounts tell us that the warrior walks a fine line between using his instruments to serve or to destroy what is true and good. As I said before, no one would argue that a pistol, a sword, and a fly rod express the same degree of refinement of intent, even though they are all beautiful to the eye and fall on the same continuum. But historically and psychologically, the process of a man's emergence begins on the primitive end. Our first impulse is to acquire the magic sword and to exercise raw power. Then, if we are fortunate, something less violent — such as a fly rod — may replace our original weapons of choice. But not long ago, we were hunters, and our livelihood depended on our ability to use weapons to feed our families and to defend our hearths. When survival becomes the goal, violence becomes a virtue. And so, most of us still enter the process at the primitive end of the continuum, remembering the path our ancestors trod.

It may even be necessary for most men to begin as warriors and hunters and to express their lust for power in a context designed to accommodate it. Perhaps only then can we lay aside the weapons that supported us in our ascent and turn back to honor the mothers and lovers who have waited for our return. But until then, we will surely overlook the signs of their heartache and decline.

Roger's mother, Joyce, was like my second mother, and she loved me, I'm sure, like I was her son. Whenever I'd visit her, she would show immense interest in my activities. She was always so kind and generous to me that I never saw the signs of suicidal depression.

But one day, soon after the Nolens moved to Colorado, she took Roger's .22 pistol out into the woods, put it to her head, and shot herself. The instrument that Roger had enjoyed for so many years became the instrument of his mother's undoing.

A few months after she died, I went to Texas to visit my family. It just so happened that Roger was visiting briefly to help his dad and uncle take care of the business that they had co-owned for many years. We didn't talk much about his mom's death — it was awkward — but we did fish together for several days on the Laguna Madre. It was an unforgettable summer when the small trout were congregated in huge schools just to the north of Green Island. Each day we fished, we caught 20 to 30 trout before the morning was over.

It was the last time we visited our hometown together. Roger's father sold the business after Roger's uncle died, and there hasn't been an occasion for us to be there at the same time. But one night before we parted, we went out driving along the levees around the floodways, as we had done as teenagers. We drove along the main canal, where we'd often shot our pistols at turtles and grackles years before, and we came to a low bridge where many of us had gone night after night during our last year in high school to talk about the future. We paused there, and he broke down. He wept openly about his mom, Benny, and others who had died untimely deaths. I was quiet and did not know what to say.

"Don't die on me, Sparrow," he pleaded tearfully.

Of course, I assured him that I would live. But claiming, and caring for what we've been given, is not as simple as it sounds for some of us. Something as outwardly simple as wielding a beautiful fly rod and making a fine cast conveys, on a deeper level, the tacit promise that we will live fully through the instrument that God has given us.

It may be that this is the greatest promise that we can ever make. And while I gladly reassured my best friend, the person I really needed to convince was myself.

Fortunately, the example that my mother set may have freed me from any inclination to resort to desperate remedies. By leaving my father, she affirmed her own life even as she presided over the death of the family as we knew it.

At 16, I was totally unaware of what was afoot. Dad and Mom had never really fought, so there was no indication that divorce was imminent. Just before she left in 1967, Hurricane Beulah hit the Lower Laguna Madre and came inland toward our hometown. The storm also dumped over 30 inches of rain in 24 hours. Meanwhile, we rode out the storm at home, listening to the trees falling all around us.

In the midst of all of this destruction, Mom and I played double solitaire on the den floor. Using the only playing cards that she and

Dad owned, we sat toe-to-toe, intensely focused on a game that mirrored a lonely struggle against the odds and against each other. There was a sense of tenderness beneath the play and a recognition of our similarities. Looking back, I think she was saying goodbye.

Of all the trees that fell that day, the tall *tepeguaje* reminded me of my mother. With its delicate leaves, it had erected a lattice-like canopy over the front yard. But under the force of the winds, the trunk had splintered, and the branches had leaned over until they touched the ground. When I returned home from school two days later, I was surprised to see that Dad had finished the work that the storm had begun. Recalling skills that he'd learned as a young man in rural Alabama, he had wielded the ax like a master woodsman and severed the trunk just above the ground.

My work with Chas Matthews began two years before my trip to the Laguna Madre. He lived in Williamsburg, and taught at my alma mater, The College of William and Mary. Even though he was my professor and dissertation chairman, he extended the hand of friendship to me as though he felt some kinship between us. I never felt comfortable seeking him out in that way. Once again, I suppose I was afraid of him rejecting me in the end. But after my midlife crisis began several years later, I turned to him to guide me through the darkest times of my life.

One day after we'd worked together for a few months, he suggested that I do some "holotropic" breathworKathy He felt that I'd gone as far as I could go in talking therapy and that the breathwork might open me to a deeper level of healing and integration. While the idea frightened me, I trusted him. So I said okay, and he set aside three hours on the next Monday to lead me through the process.

A person's home tells a lot about them — sometimes more than they would like others to know — but Chas' home offered no surprises. It was an old colonial across the street from William and Mary, nestled beneath a canopy of ancient hardwoods. There was no grass to speak of. An old white trellis covered a walkway and English ivy could be seen here and there around the trees and at the base of the house. The house had not been painted in a long time, and a bit of moss gave the white siding a hint of green. It all fit the man I'd come to know as my professor, mentor, and therapist.

He advised me to empty my bladder before we began. Little did I know that every bodily function would speed up during the lengthy breathwork session due to the increase in metabolism. As I stood in the bathroom, I noticed on the wall a photograph of a smiling Indian woman in the traditional saffron robe of a monKathy I had never seen her, but I knew from Chas' comments during earlier sessions that she was his guru — Gurumayi Chidvilasananda, the successor to Swami Muktananda. From her smile, I could see that she had a playful disposition. And further, she looked a lot like my mother.

I laid on the rug, and Chas sat cross-legged on one side of me. Before he turned on the soundtrack from *Mission*, he told me briefly that the breathwork would create an altered state of consciousness that would allow me to experience whatever I needed to experience. He said he did not know what would happen, and that he was often surprised during his own breathwork sessions. Then he asked me if it was okay if he held my arm during the process. I said "Of course," but I wondered why.

He said, "Scott, you've had plenty of out-of-body experiences. But now you need to have an in-the-body experience."

Having never done breathwork before, I didn't know what to do, nor what to expect. Chas told me to breathe rapidly and high in my chest, and in a few minutes my arms began to tingle as my blood became saturated with oxygen.

At first, I kept wondering what was supposed to happen, but somehow the breathwork dissolved this self-consciousness. After a few minutes, I was free to experience a dramatic shift in awareness and the beginning of what might be called "the deeper agenda."

Suddenly, I felt I was in a hammock, swinging wildly and dizzily in all directions.

I could barely stay in my body, but Chas' grip on my arm was just firm enough to keep me focused on the here and now.

Then the movement subsided. I was going to stay, apparently.

It was then that they came, and they were all women whom I had known. Without exception, I had hurt them, and they had hurt me, and it was time to confront those feelings. I began to weep as anger, sorrow, and grief were conjoined in a mixture that would normally have sent me fleeing for cover. But Chas whispered, "Let your warrior spirit guide you through it," so I stayed with it. Gradually, one by one, these relationships passed through me, leaving behind a sense of deep relief and forgiveness.

Toward the end, Roger's mother came. For some reason, I had never grieved her passing. But in this altered state, the past was no longer a distant memory. It was alive again, and so was she. And the tears just poured out of me. Finally, I said goodbye to the woman who had been a second mother to me. As she faded, the last person came with a force that convinced me that she was actually present.

On the night before my mother died, my stepfather, John, called me from Texas and said that I'd better come — and soon. I was surprised, because she'd been doing so well with her cancer for so long. In a few hours, I was on a plane to Houston. As fate would have it, my plane was delayed two hours due to bad weather, so I arrived in the little town of Columbus after 11:00 p.m. that night. John said that Mom had just gone to sleep, so it might be better to wait 'til morning to see her. A few hours later, the hospital called to tell us that she had died in her sleep.

Mom had told everyone, with obvious pride, "My boys are coming to see me." Chip had arrived from South Texas the previous afternoon and had spent several hours at her bedside. But I arrived too late to have those precious final moments with her.

And so, it was fitting that she would come to assist in my healing. But she had something important to take care of, first. I heard her say, "I am sorry that I hurt you." She had never said that in all of the years since she'd left the family. I responded, "It's okay, Mom. I am sorry, too."

As we made our peace and parted, white light began to fill my vision. I thought at first that the setting sun was pouring through the window onto my face. But no, it was the Holy Light coming to take her place. And then, I felt myself being born again. It was quite physical. Chas seemed to know what was happening, for he went around and sat at my head, then held my shoulders, as if to welcome me into the world. There was a pronounced physical sensation of movement upward through my head into his waiting arms.

On the day of Kathy's arrival, I awakened early with a list of things to do. I bathed and shaved more carefully than usual and took a good look at my hair. After wearing a cap every day for a month, my hair had little curls at the bottom, making me look like a balding Betty Boop. The curls will have to go, I concluded, so I added "haircut" to the list. Above that, I had written "watermelon," "wine," "pasta," and "clam sauce," in the order of my priorities.

Getting a cheap haircut in Harlingen, Texas, is easy. There are signs everywhere advertising them for as little as $3.00. The only problem is that the haircut comes with a barber who cannot speak English, and who is accustomed to completing the job in less than three minutes. That would work for me on most occasions, but given the specialness of the day, I decided to get a recommendation, so I stopped a man on the street and asked him where he got his hair cut. He pointed me in the direction of an establishment just around the corner. On the basis of one stranger's advice, I parked the car and went in.

A huge mustached man in a Mexican wedding shirt greeted me at the door and ushered me to an empty barber stool in the middle of an empty room. He squinted at my hair, and I could see that he wondered why I'd waited so long. When I told him that I would be meeting a woman at the airport, he brightened considerably, and — for my benefit — began listing the things that women love in a man. Apparently, however, his vast knowledge had not succeeded in winning his love — a woman 20 years younger, who still lived with her parents. For some reason, he could not pry her free of them. I thought it best not to analyze his methods, nor her resistance to them.

When he asked what brought me to South Texas, I told him about my fly fishing quest. Again, he launched into spirited monologue about the joys of angling — not for small fish mind you, but for giant alligator gar. On the weekends, he and his friends would set out trot-lines in local canals and then return late at night to check the lines. Paddling quietly in the dark and carrying machetes, they would hack the giant gar to death before it could struggle, and then drag its bloody and mangled body aboard their jon boat. Some of the meat they smoked, and some they sold; but regardless, they had great fun, and their friends and families treated them as heroes.

The man's unexamined confidence clearly accounted for his success as an angler, but also for his failure as a lover. While I cringed at the image of the swinging blades, the man had a passion and a con-

fidence that was infectious. He was at least willing to wield his instrument, however primitive it seemed to me. As I pondered the relative benefits and drawbacks of unquestioned self-confidence, I was startled by a friendly slap on my checks by the man's two hands.

"This is my secret weapon!" he exclaimed. "She won't have a chance," he added confidently and proceeded to rub it into my hair, as well.

The generic smell of flowers filled the room. I was horrified, but it was too late to do anything about it. I paid the man and left.

Avoiding contact with people as best I could, I drove to a nearby gas station and spent 10 minutes desperately lathering and re-lathering my face and hair.

When I hugged Kathy at the gate, the first thing she said was, "What is that smell!?"

Toward the end of my retreat on the Laguna Madre, I decided that I would purchase a new top-of-the-line rod and reel. I had the eight-weight Sage, but I felt I could use a seven-weight rod for those calmer days when a more delicate presentation could make the difference between spooking a big fish and drawing a strike.

It was not easy to call Larry at The Shop and to order the seven-weight Sage rod and the new Ross reel. Of course, I could do without it. But I knew, as well, that I would never cross the threshold into the inner sanctum of fly fishing until I surrendered my unthinking repudiation of everything fine and beautiful.

So, Kathy and I drove over to Port Isabel to pick up the new rod and reel. Larry had installed new line and backing, as well, so I was ready to fish as soon as I walked out of the store. Still feeling a little stunned over having spent nearly a thousand dollars on this outfit, I drove up the Island to try it out. As we came to the end of the pavement, several miles north of the town of South Padre Island, I put the Rodeo in four-wheel drive and headed for the bay, a half mile to the west.

Thirty minutes later, Kathy and I were wading 100 yards from the shoreline in grass-free, gin-clear water. It was getting deep enough to begin fishing, so, I stripped out some line, lifted the rod into the air, and began false casting. But as I played out more line, the loop suddenly collapsed on the water. I couldn't believe it! The new Sage SP felt like a broom stick in my hand.

But then I remembered my music teacher's words. "This is a different kind of instrument. You have to learn to fill this instrument if you want to discover what it can do."

On the heels of this memory, a dream came back to me from years before. In it, I had become lucid and realized that I was dreaming. I decided to look for the Light, so I looked around hoping to see it and to commune with it. At first, every object in the dream glowed around the edges, subtly announcing the presence of the Light. As I concentrated on a bicycle that was glowing brightly, hoping that they would dissolve into pure radiance, it promptly lost its luster and became ordinary in appearance. Growing more and more frustrated, I turned from one thing to another, only to see each object become merely itself.

Then, an unknown woman walked up to me and said, "You must first learn to love the form before you can see the Light within it."

After all these years, I realized that she and the woman on the water were one and the same. She was the one whose singular message has always been to go more deeply into my experience — to breathe deeply — and never, never to turn away. I also realized that she was the Being my mother had longed to find when she went in search of herself.

As these memories flooded in, I stood quietly admiring the beautiful rod. The blue graphite shone in the sunlight with a translucency that reminded me of the crystal wand I'd carried in that dream years before.

I retrieved some of my line, took a deep breath, and lifted it into the air once again. This time, I watched the line as it passed overhead. Following it, and never losing sight of it, I could feel my body adjusting to the rod's unfamiliar rhythm. In the crosswind, the loop made a spinning circle that finally remained aloft.

A beautiful instrument makes it possible for us to express the unrevealed essence of who we are. Composed of the elements of this world, it also keeps us grounded — ever cognizant of the debt that we owe the feminine spirit who presides over this world of form.

Thus, it should come as no surprise that somewhere along the way, we turn back and honor with feeling the one who ushered us into this world, even though she may have hurt us or faltered in her own quest for meaning.

A beautiful instrument also brings us closer to the Creator, whose perfectly suited instruments we are. For who, other than us, can do spirit's bidding in this world? And what more beautiful wand could there ever be to transmit the Light of the soul?

Wednesday, August 7, 2002, morning
Arroyo City, Texas

I Imagine that I'm Improving

Raised lesions began to develop on both sides of my foot, and pus-filled blisters arose alongside and atop the lesions. Since I had been to the doctor on Monday, I thought that these changes indicated that the problem was "coming to the surface." I decided to help the process by lancing the blisters and the lesions with my fly tying bodkin needle. Although pus streamed out of the blisters, nothing much came from the angry red lesions, which puzzled me. I also thought that the recurrent fevers were signs that the infection was on the decline. Meanwhile, I kept my foot wrapped in gauze and covered with socks, hoping — at least consciously — that the situation was improving.

Kathy was scheduled to take over a charter on Thursday, so I offered to go along. She rejected the offer at first, but then agreed that she needed my help in finding the fish. To keep the wound out of the seawater, I planned to wear a stocking foot hip wader and then put a larger wading boot over my foot.

10

The End is Everywhere

Arroyo City, Texas - early August 1997

"Time flies so fast after youth is past that we cannot accomplish one half the many things we have in mind...The only safe and sensible plan is to make other things give way to the essentials, and the first of these is fly fishing."
Theodore Gordon

The cottage had one large room and a porch with a bed. When I moved in at the beginning of my stay on the water, I took the porch for myself and slept beside a window that afforded me a view of the Arroyo and the boat docKathy In exchange, Ryan gladly took custody of two full-size beds and the TV in the great room, and slept alone without complaint.

Upon awakening in the middle of the night, I would sometimes see a screech owl sitting on the chain link fence in the lamp light or a night heron that perched atop the boathouse, and I would often spot coyotes or a pack of raccoons searching for food across the water, their eyes glowing from the dock lights. And, on some nights, I would awaken with a start to a deep thrumming sound that shook the window panes. Over the sill would appear a massive metal structure adorned with red and green and yellow lights, and topped with a white beam that cut through the darkness like a glowing saber. The tower of the tugboat would briefly loom above the trees and the cottage as it passed

144

slowly westward, pushing its cargo through the darkness toward Port Harlingen 15 miles away. In my half-sleep, it seemed that the tower was the only stationary thing, and that the trees and the cottage and my bed were moving slowly eastward toward the Laguna Madre — away

from everything bright and metallic and harsh, and where everything living must eventually go.

This recurring nighttime surprise brought to mind another series of awakenings during my preadolescent years. During that time, I would often wake up in the middle of the night to the sight of a shadowy figure standing just outside my window. Too terrified to cry out, I would watch wide-eyed as the intruder quietly slid the window open. Then, as always, I would hear the reassuring sound of my brother's voice.

"Be quiet! It's me!" Offering no further explanation, he would crawl through the window onto my bed, roll over me onto the floor, and then get up and collapse in his bed against the far wall. When he entered the house this way, he had usually been to Mexico dancing and drinking. For obvious reasons, he preferred entering the house through the window rather than through the front door. I don't know how my parents accounted for his presence in the morning. I suppose they had to overlook some things in the course of raising six children.

Chip seemed to be having a good time. He was 16, and he had begun dating a stunningly beautiful girl, Linda. She was known throughout the area for her beauty, and Chip was obviously smitten. But like most extraordinarily attractive people, Linda kept her options open.

Then one day, Chip asked Linda to go out the following Friday night, but she told him that she had already made plans. It was obvious that she had a date with someone else. When Friday night came, I recall that Chip received a phone call in the middle of the night from a friend whose dad owned the local mortuary. Gary had been driving their ambulance that night and had been called to the scene of an accident. Linda and her date had been involved in a head-on collision. Her date had survived, but she had died instantly.

I recall seeing my brother lying quietly on his bed during the days following Linda's death. The unspoken thought that must have tormented him was, If only she'd liked me more. We never spoke about it, but it seemed to me that Chip changed a bit from that time, leaving behind some of his boyish enthusiasm and developing a harder shell around his feelings. It was a method that seemed to offer him a bit of sanctuary in a world where the end is everywhere.

While Chip and I shared a small bedroom until he left for college, we rarely touched upon the deeper matters that trouble young men and which make for lifelong wounds. But there have been moments of intimacy scattered through our lives. One day during the time of my mother's long battle with cancer, he and I went out to get a burger. Somehow, her terminal illness opened the door to the past, and we began talking about our parents' divorce 20 years before. It may seem odd, but we had never discussed it at all. He had already left for college, after all, and our times together were limited to summers and holidays.

As we began talking about our own experiences, we discovered that we had taken turns spending nights with Dad in a pathetic little motel where he went to stay after Mom told him that it was over. We discovered, too, that we had both held our father while he wept — trying to support him as we, too, were being left. Chip and I could go no further without breaking down in that little greasy spoon. True to form, we quickly reigned in our feelings and finished our meals, but not before giving way to feelings that we'd never revealed to anyone — feelings about the end of our family as we'd known it.

Before Ryan departed for Virginia, he and I left the cottage one morning at daybreak and headed north from the mouth of the Arroyo toward Woody's Hole. My limited success fishing with Chip a couple of days earlier prompted me to return for another chance at a big trout. I still hoped that a trophy fish could be caught somewhere around that shallow entrance to the West Bay.

We anchored the boat on the edge of the channel, and stepped ever-so carefully into the murky transitional water between the channel and the clear flats. Stingrays loved this muddy place, but Ryan was not worried in the least. He had petted rays in a special hands-on exhibit back home, so he considered the rays his friends. Regardless, no friend takes kindly to being stepped on, so I took his hand and made him walk slowly beside me. As we dragged our feet along the soft bottom, the rich odors of decomposing marine life bubbled to the surface.

"Dad, what's that horrid smell?!" Ryan asked.

Rather than going into a lengthy discourse on the matter, I said simply, "That is the smell of the Laguna Madre." Knowing that he found the odor disgusting, I decided to take it a little further, as fathers often foolishly do. "I love it, don't you? I mean, if they made a cologne that smelled like this, I would wear it every day back home to remind me of this place." Even though I was exaggerating, I did like the smell.

"Oh, Dad, don't say that!" At that moment, he vomited, spilling his Cheerios into the source of the smell, answering its insult in kind.

I felt bad about having pushed him over the edge, and I apologized. But vomiting came easily to Ryan; it was no big deal. He kept on going and was soon distracted by the barnacle-encrusted treasure that lay strewn across the spoil banKathy While I fished unsuccess-

fully, he discovered bobbers half buried in the piled-up seagrass, a fisherman's cap, an old styrofoam ice chest that had floated up on the bank at high tide, and a crude chair made of two-by-fours that he treated as a little throne. Enchanted by the treasure, Ryan soon overlooked the smell, and I knew enough not to mention it again.

On the water, death is everywhere. Dead birds litter the spoil banks, and mullet lie bloated and insignificant along every shoreline. The bay teems with life, and so death, too, occupies a prominent place there.

Of all things living on the Lower Laguna Madre, the fisherman is the presence most unnatural and godlike. As one surveys the bay in all directions, virtually nothing but small boats and wading fishermen alter the seamless relationship between water, sand, and sky. Just being there awakens an eerie sense of dominion that can put distance between ourselves and the sobering truth of our own mortality. If we succeed at fishing, it pushes us even further away from the sense of death. For when we succeed, we hold the fish's fate in our hands. We stand over our quarry dealing death or mercy on a whim. But too often, we come up empty-handed. Then, if we are open to it, the life and death that surrounds us begins whispering to us through feelings and smells that we cannot fully decipher. Like the fish, we feel that we move just ahead of an unrevealed Presence who holds our fate in his hands.

Most of us, if honest, feel anxious about something over which we have little control. Death and love and God and the capriciousness of Nature become interchangeable in the simple psychology of fear: They are all unpredictable. The tinge of anxiety attached to everything uncontrollable is probably what makes us want to claim a kind of token power over something as elusive and wild as a fish. Although we may possess little fear of stingrays, or of drowning, or of lightning — or of the many other things that can suddenly go wrong on the water — most of us are afraid of something. From this, we may recoil, believing perhaps, that we have successfully isolated ourselves from what disturbs our peace. But the avoidance of anything eventually spills over into everything. Then we may wonder why the passion that once gave our lives color is receding from us, often while we are still young men.

If Chip recoiled somewhat after Linda died, I took one of many steps backwards when I was about five years old. My grandfather lived half a mile down the street, and he had a swimming pool that we'd visit on foot almost every summer day. But between our house and his swimming pool lay a gauntlet of unpredictable dogs and people. First, there was old Mr. Wilson who often yelled at us for taking shortcuts through his yard. Roger left a burning bag of dog shit by his front door one Halloween night, which did nothing to improve relations between us. The image of Mr. Wilson stomping on that bag brings a smile to my face, even now 45 years later. Farther along, a yellow dog whose name I have since repressed lay in wait unceasingly for every kid and car that entered his territory. And in between, set back under the trees was Jack's house which, by itself, posed no particular threat to us. But when Jack's dad came home, and began drinking, the older kids knew enough to stay away.

One day I went there with my brother, who was Jack's age and a good friend of his. I thought I would be safe with my older brother, but I was wrong. I had a cold, and my nose was running. Jack's dad was home, and he seemed friendly enough at first, but I did not understand alcoholism back then. So, when he suddenly exploded in rage over my disgusting appearance, and my constant snorting, I ran out of the house crying uncontrollably, and did not stop running until I was safely back home. After this incident, I developed a nervous habit of snorting loudly that frustrated my father and brother whenever we went hunting. Anything and anyone could hear me coming a hundred yards away, but at least my nose would never run again — if I could help it.

It was eerie when I discovered recently that Jack's dad had fallen in love with the Laguna Madre in his later years, and had fished there as often as he could. Stories about his transformation began trickling down through Chip and Dad and other friends who had known him years back when he drank and raged at his first wife and his children. Something had healed him. I saw him fishing alone on a couple of occasions during my month on the water. I would pass by him, waving, knowing that he had no idea who I was, or what he had once done to me.

I have heard that on one occasion while Dale was fishing alone, he hooked a giant trout and managed to bring it alongside his boat after a lengthly battle. Looking down, he saw a trout that was well over 36 inches long. It may have have been the largest speckled trout ever caught, but as he went to net the giant fish, the hook came loose. Like Moses who witnessed the Promised Land, but was forbidden to enter in, Dale must have felt uniquely blessed and punished as he watched the fish swim away.

My father enjoyed a particularly close relationship with Dale during the final years of his life. Through Dad, I began to hear about

Dale's remarkable generosity and about his humor. I marveled that the man who once raged at me as a child had undergone such a metamorphosis.

All of us can recall encounters with alcoholics or unchained dogs or divorce or the sudden death of loved ones. It is a natural thing to take refuge from such memories, but these defensive tactics impose limits on the risks that we are willing to take in the pursuit of our dreams, including catching big fish. We might scoff at the suggestion that a deep loss or an early trauma could have anything to do with our inability to connect with wild fish. But then we would be mistaken.

When I was about 20, I dreamed that I took off in a small fighter-bomber during World War II. My copilot and I were the only men aboard the plane, and we headed eastward across the English Channel and over the mainland of France.

Somewhere along the way, we were hit by enemy fire and went down. I do not remember any pain or suffering, only the experience of standing outside the plane, looking dispassionately upon my dead body. I somehow knew that I had lived to be 21 years of age, had known a great deal about spiritual truths, but had done little to advance my development. As I made this assessment, I saw a man approaching on foot from the north. I recognized him as Rick, one of my friends in this lifetime. He said, "Come on, Scott. It is time to go bacKathy" I followed him down a road and over a hill. I knew that we were heading toward our next lifetime.

I have dreaded plane flight for most of my adult life. Even though I fly frequently, I never seem to get used to it, and I will do just about anything to avoid it. Ironically, my life experience has done nothing to dispel this fear, for I come from a family of plane crash victims.

My father — who was a B-29 navigator and bombardier during World War II — crashed while returning from the longest bombing mission ever flown before that time. On the way back to Ceylon (Sri Lanka) from Palembang, Sumatra, his plane could not access one of its fuel tanks, and it ran out of gas. Consequently, the bomber had to be ditched over water. The survivors waited in life rafts in Japanese-infested waters until a British ship rescued them 36 hours later. My father's friend from Tennessee — who had sat beside him as they braced themselves for impact — died in the crash. My father still wonders, as anyone would: Why him and not me?

I discovered that my stepfather, John, crash landed before the War during flight training. The crash effectively ended his hopes for becoming a pilot for the U.S., so he went to Canada to pursue his dream. As an RAF pilot based in England during the War, he flew a B-17 in the European theater. But he left my mother — his fiancé — behind. In his absence, she met and fell in love with my father, who came to Texas to do his flight training before leaving for the War. My dad washed out, too, due to vision problems, but he accepted the position of navigator-bombardier and completed his training in the States. Ironically, John came back into my mom's life after his wife died years later and served as the catalyst for Mom's decision to leave my father after 27 years of marriage. He had gone full circle and won her bacKathy

When I was about 25, my sister's husband Tony crashed his homebuilt "cassette racer" at a Midwest air show after having served a full stint as a carrier pilot in Vietnam. He died on impact as his tiny plane dove into the ground after losing power on take off.

Shortly thereafter, Judy went on tour of Europe as a way to deal with her grief over Tony's death. While staying with friends in Spain, she met her husband-to-be, Jim, who proposed to her before she left for the States. As Judy flew home, undecided about whether to accept Jim's proposal, her Iberia airliner undershot the runway upon landing at Logan Airport in Boston. It hit the swamp, and the fuselage broke in half as it slid to a halt. Miraculously, there was no explosion or fire, and everyone survived. Covered with mud, but unharmed, Judy jumped out of the side of the ruptured fuselage, mentally saying yes to Jim's proposal and to a second chance at life.

Chip enjoyed six years without incident as an Air Force pilot. He can recount stories of near-disaster, as most pilots can. But when it comes to staying in the air, Chip stands apart as the most fortunate flyer in the family. Not surprisingly, he is the only one who has shown much interest in flying as a civilian.

Several years ago, Chip bought the plane of his dreams — a small, "homebuilt," experimental plane capable of doing aerobatics. He operates the RV-4 with the utmost of care, and he takes no chances. He recently told me, "There are three reasons pilots crash: They go too slow, they fly too low, or they fly into weather." He went on to add in a quiet, matter-of-fact tone that if your engine quits on take off, then there's nothing you can do about that, of course. In other words, you perish knowing that you did nothing wrong.

If my fears about life have coalesced into a singular aversion to flying, Chip's insecurities obviously have found their expression in other ways. I am sure that he would say that he is not "afraid" of fly fishing, but he has consistently refused to take up the sport on our home waters, and I often wonder why. In my efforts to be my brother's keeper, I have tried to convert him over the years, knowing how much he would enjoy it. I have used everything from gentle persuasion to outright insults, only to find him doggedly unyielding. I have loaned him my rods and have offered him my flies to no avail. I finally realized that the harder I tried, the more he resisted. Chastened by years of failure, I finally resorted to a kind of strategic silence, thinking that my fly fishing successes on the water would finally win him over.

One morning several years ago, I thought we'd finally had the experience that would convert him to fly fishing. Chip, Dad, my nephew, Spencer, and I went out at daybreak onto the east flats of the Laguna Madre. We stopped only a few hundred yards short of Padre Island, where the water is only about a foot deep and the bottom is hard packed sand. The wind was dead calm, and cruising fish could be seen in all directions pushing subtle "v" wakes. But catching them was another matter. Given the calm conditions, the fish spooked at the slightest disturbance, so as Chip, Dad, and Spencer began casting their spoons and topwater plugs, they were greeted with the noisy swirls of departing fish.

Yet, the conditions were perfect for fly fishing. Over the next hour and a half, the fly rod performed like a magic wand. Casting a tiny bendback that hit the water noiselessly, I proceeded to catch nine fish, including four reds and three trout. I also managed to land two ladyfish, or "skipjack," which fight like a baby tarpon and provide spectacular aerial displays. I spent half of the time on my knees, with my head low to the water, to keep from spooking the approaching fish. Some of my casts were "far and fine," but most were short, as the fish would often swim right up to me. Meanwhile, Dad, Chip, and Spencer caught a total of one redfish on their spinning lures. Chip stopped fishing altogether after a while and just stood with his rod over his shoulder, watching.

But even that day did not convert him.

During my retreat, Chip spent most of his days at home. Just before I arrived, he and his wife, Sandi, flew to Mexico City to celebrate his 50th birthday. There he contracted an illness that frustrated the doctors and kept him laid up for almost six weeks after returning home. After bouts of recurrent fever and diarrhea, Chip looked tired and older, and he hinted that he feared he might have a more serious ailment — something perhaps life threatening, something that had nothing to do with the trip south. Knowing how such fears can flourish in isolation, I encouraged him to come to join me at the cottage, if for nothing else but to sit on the water and enjoy the sunsets. But he stayed close to home, anxiously waiting to hear the latest results from his doctors.

Finally, toward the end of my month-long retreat, he recovered sufficiently enough to join me just when Kathy arrived from Virginia to spend the last couple of weeks with me.

It was an important turning point in my search for big trout. Cecil had just learned that some big trout had been spotted near a place called Dunkin's Channel. Time was running out. I was both relieved to find this out and anxious that I'd have to leave before I could succeed in my quest for a trophy trout.

Cecil, Chip, Kathy, and I left at daybreak in my boat and turned south at the mouth of the Arroyo. We boated along the Intracoastal toward Dunkin's Channel, about five miles to the south. Actually, the channel was a mere depression about a foot deeper than the surrounding flats, running westward from and perpendicular to the Intracoastal Waterway, and terminating about half a mile to the west. A large house built on stilts by wealthy banker Dial Dunkin faces the channel and marks the spot where we had to take a hard right.

Along the north side of this shallow channel were some spoil banks created years ago by a petroleum company that needed deeper water to gain access to drilling sites out in the shallow West Bay. Only the fading trail of this exploratory venture remained.

"This is the place where Steve caught the winning trout," Cecil said. He was referring to a friend who had caught the biggest trout in the Texas International Fishing Tournament just a week before. According to Cecil, Steve had fished all morning with his wife and had been taking a lunch break aboard his boat. As he ate a sandwich, he noticed the 30-inch trout cruising by. He grabbed his fly rod and made a perfect cast to a hungry fish.

"It's a tidal phenomenon," Cecil went on to say. "Steve says that sometimes he'll see nothing when he gets here. And then, as the tides start moving, big tails begin popping up everywhere."

As we looked to the northwest across the west side, an expanse of calm clear water littered with clumps of floating grass stretched out before us. If the trout were tailing, we'd be able to see them.

Chip and Cecil waded north toward the second spoil bank that was about 100 yards north of Dunkin's Channel. I walked behind with Kathy, who was still nervous about stingrays and who had only fished one day thus far since arriving. I knew she still needed advice and assistance with her gear.

Outfitted with tiny walkie talkies, Chip and Cecil kept in touch enough to tell me that they saw nothing moving in the shallow water. They crossed over the spoil bank and stood watching the water for tails on the north side of the little island.

Meanwhile, I went slower than I usually did, keeping just ahead and to the left of Kathy. I found myself studying the water with almost trancelike concentration. Even though Chip and Cecil had just waded through the same water, I had little choice but to hope that some fish were moving in behind them.

Then I saw something that puzzled me at first. The black outline of a fish's back stuck out of the water within three feet of the spoil bank's shoreline. Could it be a trout, I wondered? I waded ever so carefully toward it, but it disappeared before I could move into casting range. I then saw another anomaly upwind from me: a barely perceptible movement like a snake on top of the water. My brain processed this as the signature of a trout, but I talked myself out of it. That is, until I got closer and saw that it was, indeed, a sizable trout sauntering through a school of nervous mullet.

I called Kathy's attention to the trout's presence, and she, too, saw it snaking through the glassy water before it disappeared from view. I cast my popper in its general vicinity, but I lost track of where the fish was, and I was unable to draw a strike. It was also possible, I realized, that the trout had been feeding at night under the waxing moon. In a week or so, the moon would be full. I cursed my luck, for I realized that I was finally zeroing in on the location of big trout during a time when they'd be feeding at night. My trip might be over by the time they resumed feeding during the daylight hours.

I got on the radio and told Cecil and Chip about what we'd just seen. Minutes later, they were heading back to the boat, not to scope out our find, but to leave. They were unconvinced that there was any merit in sticking around this place. Chip is usually in a hurry to move on, and he covers a lot of water looking for concentrations of fish. His style works for him, but I often feel rushed when we fish together.

When we got into the boat, I told them again about seeing the big trout. Cecil laughed and asked me if I was sure it wasn't a mullet-inspired fantasy. Even though it was in good fun, I knew that he doubted that we'd seen two big trout. Being new to the bay, Kathy's observations carried no weight, so we left the place, harboring different views about what had just happened. They thought the water was empty. I believed we had simply failed to acknowledge what was there. I looked at Kathy and I knew that we shared the same conviction — to return here as soon as we could.

Over the years it has occurred to me that anglers freely impose their own subjective realities upon the water, and that we can only see what our beliefs will allow us to see. Few of us are fully open to what is before us. This was driven home to me a couple of years ago while fishing on the glorious West Branch of the Delaware. The river was discolored and swollen from rains, and bits of moss from the reservoir above the dam filled the river. I was there, so I fished; but it was one of those times when I wished I'd chosen a different week to drive 11 hours to fish my favorite northeast stream.

I noticed some trout rising to a Baetis hatch, so I used a size 20 parachute blue-winged olive. It was a good choice, for I quickly missed two rises, and then broke off my 7x tippet on another trout. At midday, I climbed the bank to the parking lot and ate my sandwich on the tailgate of the Rodeo. Meanwhile, two men came up another trail from the river. I'd fished a different portion of the river, so they must have thought I'd just arrived.

"How'd you do?" I asked.

"About as good as you're going to do. Terribly. Don't waste your time," one said conclusively.

I said nothing to contradict the man, knowing that it would either embarrass him or convince him that I was a liar. A few minutes later, I went back down to the river. The trout were still there, rising in a feeding lane near the banKathy I cast my tiny fly ahead of a rise, and the fish rose to it without hesitation. A few minutes later, I released a beautiful, butter-colored, 18-inch brown.

I remarked to myself how we see only what we wish to see, and how often our conclusions about the water merely serve to protect us from a sense of failure and a greater truth. Rather than feeling superior in that moment, I wondered how often that I was the one clinging to the illusion.

We stopped at two other places on the way back to the cottage. By the time we finally returned around midday, I had caught and released one tailing redfish, and that was it. Cecil left the cottage immediately, for he had to return to Port Isabel. I expected Chip to take a nap, visit with us the rest of the day, and then to go out again in the morning. But he left the cottage with a vague promise to come back down again soon.

Kathy and I were a little puzzled and disappointed that the get-together with Cecil and Chip had ended so abruptly. We napped for a while, and I awoke in a deep depression. In giving voice to my feelings, I realized that my brother and I had done what we had done most of our adult lives — avoided the opportunity to come closer and to share our affection on common ground. I felt that I reached out more often than he did, and the results always seemed the same.

Later, I realized that I was probably recalling on an emotional level the day that Cecil's brother, Johnny, died 41 years earlier. On that fateful Sunday, Chip and Cecil had planned to ride Cecil's horse after church, but when they arrived at the stable, they found that Johnny had already left with the horse. Several hours later, Cecil's father brought Cecil to the house, and told us that Johnny had been hit by a car while riding his horse. He left Cecil with us and hurried to the hospital. Chip, Cecil, and I sat on the sofa in awkward silence, awaiting word. Later that evening, the news came that Johnny had died.

I was seven at the time, and Johnny was 13, but he had been my best friend other than Roger. He was a different kind of friend, more of a mother and a father wrapped up into one — what Robert Bly might call a "mother-father mentor." He delighted in me, and I loved him more than God, whom I didn't really know. He never said an unkind thing to me, and he let me hit him and tickle him as much as I wanted. For some reason, I didn't cry when he died, and my parents did not take me to his funeral. But I have wept since, realizing that Johnny was such a gift to me — as, I suppose, I was to him. He was more than good: He was anointed by a great spirit that everyone who knew him could feel. The little boy in me still misses him.

I don't recall that Chip, Cecil, and I ever talked about our feelings that day. Cecil's father came to get him that evening, and everything else is a blur. And now, it seemed that so much of our lives had passed us by, with long silences filling the empty spaces.

Wednesday, August 7, 2002, evening
Arroyo City, Texas

I Desire to Live

That night, I laid down on the floor, propped my foot up, and considered all that had happened since the stingray "hit" five days earlier. I realized that I was not getting any better, and that I had probably not yet been treated properly for the infection. It was becoming clear that I had stood in the way of my recovery. So, finally, in the spirit of trying to do my part, I put some music on and laid back down. Within minutes, tears were streaming. Remembering the dream about having lost so much, a sense of grief gripped me as it had in the dream, but this time, I stayed with it. In the next hour, I grieved my son's absence from my life, love too often ended on principle, hawks and women released too soon, and brothers grown much too distant — all bound together with a single black ribbon of regret. And first among the losses was the child that Kathy and I would never have together.

The voice of singer Karen Mattheson[21] carried me into the dark mass of life unlived.

> *There are waves of forgiveness and waves of regret,*
> *And the first waves of true love I'll never forget.*
> *In the meadow that morning as I wandered alone*
> *There were green waves of yearning for life*
> *Still unknown.*

---

[21] *Secret Garden: Once in a Red Moon.* 2002. Norway: Universal Music.

Kathy came up at one point and saw that I had been going through something. "Having some feelings?" she asked.

I nodded, but said nothing. Closing my eyes, I went further into it, eventually finding that beneath the grief was something that, for too long, had been in precious short supply — a willingness to live. I felt it fill the spaces left vacant by the departing sadness and for the first time since the stingray drove its point homeward, I felt a deep desire to live.

11

Fear of Flying

Arroyo City, Texas - early August 1997

"We have no reason to mistrust our world, for it is not against us. If it has terrors, they are our own terrors." [22]
Rainier Rilke

Trying to shake the gloomy feelings, I suggested to Kathy that we pack our gear into the Shoal Cat and head back to Dunkin's Channel in the darKathy "Let's spend the night there, and fish before the sun rises." It sounded romantic and exciting, offering a respite from the dark feelings. Always game for a new adventure, and oblivious to what was resurfacing in me, Kathy readily agreed.

After packing the boat with food and overnight gear, we headed down the Arroyo about 11:00 that night, using the Q-beam and the moonlight to find the way. As we emerged from the shelter of land and entered the open water, the wind grew stronger. We knew it would settle down by early morning, and we hoped that I would be able to cast a fly before daybreaKathy But having chosen to embark on our journey so early in the night, we had no choice but to suffer the windy conditions that would prevail for many more hours.

When we turned to the south at the mouth of the Arroyo for the run to Dunkin's Channel, the 25-mph south wind became a 45- to 50-

---

[22] Rilke, R. M. 2000. *Ibid.*

163

mph wind in our face. It was disheartening and a bit frightening to plow through white-capped waves in the darkness on our way to Dunkin's Channel.

My confidence was failing. What was I doing out here? I wasn't sure why I'd jumped at the opportunity to return to Dunkin's Channel in the middle of the night under such hostile conditions. Twice I pulled the boat to a stop and conferred with Kathy. Each time, she was ready to go on, but she left it up to me. "Why is it always up to

me?" I finally yelled above the wind. I was taking it out on her. She sat quietly, knowing that something was really wrong.

"Whatever you need to do is okay with me," she said with deep conviction. She, at least, was not operating out of some unconscious pain.

We got all the way to Dunkin's Channel. The Dunkin house was aflame with light like a beacon to lost souls, but no one appeared to be there. Looking west down the shallow channel, we could see the light from a single lantern. Another boat was anchored out there, spending the night as we'd planned to do. I wondered, What the hell is wrong with him? I slowly turned the boat around, and said, "This is crazy. I can't do this." Kathy laid her hand on my shoulder as I throttled the engine and ran with the wind back to the mouth of the Arroyo.

Chip and I were close as younger brothers, but age and geographical distance has a way of converting intimacy into civility, and affection into polite respect. For years, hunting afforded us a common ground. On one memorable day when I was 19, we killed three bucks north of Rio Grande City. Chip still talks about that day, but the memory brings me no pleasure. I was sitting alone when the buck came out onto the *sindera* — the ranch road that cut through the heavy South Texas brush. I shot him as he stood looking at me, and the Winchester .243 slug broke his back, mortally wounding him. I saw him struggling to reach the brush, so I ran down the *sindera*, stopping to shoot again and again, trying to finish him off. It was only when I had come within 100 feet of him that I finally killed him. The crudeness of his death took me over the edge of a precipice where I'd been poised all my life. As Chip went on to become a master deer hunter with a wall of trophies, and wielded a spin rod in pursuit of redfish and trout, I left hunting and spin fishing behind in favor of fly fishing. Due to the erosion of our common interests, and the 1800 miles that eventually separated us, we did what most men do who have less to do together: We drifted apart.

We arrived back at the cottage around midnight and went to bed without further conversation. Around 4:30, I awoke and discovered that the strange mood had passed, and that I was eager to return to Dunkin's Channel. Kathy and I were on the water before sunrise and arrived at the narrow channel well before dawn. Kathy was still uncomfortable wading among stingrays, so she sat aboard the boat and meditated beside a lantern, while I slipped overboard with my fly rod and waded away from the boat. As I started casting my popper into the darkness, I looked back and saw Kathy's face illuminated by the lantern, growing smaller as I headed south into Rattlesnake Bay. The sun slowly revealed an unbroken, glassy expanse of crystal clear water to the north, interrupted here and there with mats of floating dead grass, and posing the kind of challenge that only a fly fisher armed with a weedless topwater can hope to meet. It was a classic summer scene.

As the sun rose higher, half a dozen fish appeared just above the glassy surface, moving slowly southward. Obviously, they had been foraging in the foot-deep water by night and were on their way toward the deeper water of Dunkin's Channel. The exposed backs and tails, and the sauntering, snakelike movement told me that they were all trout from six to eight pounds. It was what I had been searching for. In the calm conditions, however, I soon found that any noise whatsoever would cause the fish to turn away or submerge. I stalked one fish after another and failed to hook even the first one. The problem in almost every case was my presentation, which had to be perfect and then some. Casting to two crossing fish, I "ambushed" both of them by pulling the fly toward their paths. They reacted violently to this unnatural intrusion and swam quickly away, pushing a distinctive "V" across the shallow flat. I "turned" three others by slipping on the soft bottom and making too much noise. Finally, when I had the perfect opportunity — a head-on approach shot — I dropped the fly right where it needed to be and the fish simply disappeared.

I always prefer to err in the direction of blaming myself for my angling failures. Too often, it seems, fly fishers will fault the fish or the fly without realizing that the problem — and the solution — is much closer at hand. Hewitt's statement, "Your fly is all right; the trouble is on the other end of the rod" is a rule that I live by. It might make us feel better by blaming something other than ourselves, but by doing so, we disavow all that we can do to make a difference.

It's tempting to blame a trout's lack of response to her lack of hunger. Large speckled trout may not be hungry when they're digesting a big mullet, but they can still be enticed to hit a fly. Bud Rowland — who has caught the largest speckled trout ever taken on a fly rod — once told me, "I can get a big trout to eat almost any time." In support of his bold contention, he once caught a 10-pound, 11-ounce trout on his tiny Numero Uno fly, and when he lifted the trout out of the water, he could see the tail of a foot-long mullet lodged in its gullet. What made that fish eat? Was it responding from lingering hunger or a reflex action more akin to aggression? The latter, more likely.

Of course, hunger may determine whether a trout keeps attacking your fly again and again. When a big trout hits, she may give up

after a single, halfhearted nip at the fly, or she may pursue your fly relentlessly, hitting it repeatedly even after feeling the prick of the hoo-
Kathy

It's also popular to accuse big trout of being finicky. Even though big trout are wary and often hard to catch, they aren't as selective as you might think, and they're not too proud to take tiny flies. While a big mullet may be the meal of choice, big trout are, to some extent, opportunistic predators and will often attack whatever crosses their paths. Although every expert fly fisher that I know swears by his own favorite trout patterns, most of them also agree that big trout can be provoked into striking a fly of virtually any description — but only if the fly is presented impeccably. This is probably why the flies that work for one fly fisher often bear little resemblance to the preferred patterns of other successful fly fishers.

The trout disappeared an hour after sunrise, so I returned to the boat and sat with Kathy, enjoying the sights and sounds of early morning on the flats. The southeast sea breeze was just beginning to stir, bringing the pungent smell of Padre Island's flora across the flats. Nearby reddish egrets danced around hunting "canopy style" — with their wings outstretched — while a great blue heron looked upon their antics with an air of disdain.

Later that day, as we sipped our coffee on the dock, I began to speak tentatively about what had happened the previous night. I realized that my brother and I were anxious about different things, and that our resistances were keeping us from finding a new common ground. I dreaded the thing he loved — flying — and he avoided fly fishing for some reason that I could not fathom. As we were nearing the end of my fly fishing retreat, I decided that the next step in my quest had to take place above the earth — where I was afraid to go. Knowing that Chip could assist me in this challenge, I called him that evening and asked him if he would take me flying. In exchange, I challenged him to join me on the water with only a fly rod.

I was surprised by how enthusiastically he accepted the challenge. Later, I found that virtually everyone had somehow excused themselves from going up in his new plane. Dad arrived late for his first flight, and Judy's husband, Jim, was deemed too large to crawl into the back seat of the tiny plane. Sandi said that she would go up — someday. His son, Spencer, had been up only once and had gotten air sick in the process. So Chip's enthusiasm probably had much more to do with wanting anyone to fly with him, than wanting to fly fish with me.

Chip elected to fly fish with me before we could find time to go up in his plane. At least we would survive the first stage of the process, I thought.

Instead of going out in the boat, we decided to wade into the Laguna Madre from the east side of Padre Island on the hard-packed sandy bottom. There, wading and casting would be easier, and we could spread out as much as we needed. Chip, Kathy, and I drove down to Padre Island early in the morning and parked on the paved road at a remote place called Coyote Hill — a large dune overlooking the spot where he and I had caught so many big fish 20 years before that we could barely drag them back across the dunes. Coyotes could often be seen patrolling the edge of the bay for fish and rodents, and that's how the area got its name.

When we got out of the car, the wind almost knocked us over. It already was up to about 20 mph. I knew that I could handle the wind with my eight-weight, but I had serious concerns about Kathy and Chip. Kathy was game, but I could see that Chip was worried.

"Are you ready to do it?" I asked.

Chip paused and said, "It's your call."

Knowing that it was up to me, I wanted them to have a good experience. Fly fishing was hard enough without having to deal with strong winds.

"Let's go get some breakfast," I said. I could see the relief on his face.

Early the next morning, Chip called me at my sister's house where Kathy and I had stayed the night. It was 6:30, and Kathy and I had just begun to have our first cup of coffee.

"There's just a slight cross wind," Chip said. "If we get to the airport soon, we might be able to fly."

I got out of bed and met him at the door a few minutes later. On the way to the airport, we called the airport recording that updated the wind and weather every few minutes. The wind was still only seven knots, but it was blowing across the runway and rising steadily.

Chip checked and rechecked every aspect of his plane. Finally, he opened the tiny cockpit and strapped me in the back seat. Even though we were only two feet apart, we wore radios so we could communicate over the roar of the powerful Lycoming engine. The cockpit was so small that my feet stretched forward around his seat. He told me that I would have to move them later so he could reach the lever to lower the flaps for landing. No problem! We taxied down the runway and ran over a partially recessed runway light. The noise of hitting it alarmed me: "What was that?!" I asked with obvious panic in my voice. I could hear Chip chuckle over the radio. "It's just a runway light. It's okay." We turned to face the expanse of tarmac stretching out before us. Then Chip feathered the engine and spoke to me.

"The cross wind is at seven knots, and it's rising fast. Take off and landing in a crosswind with a tail wheel is always a little tricky, but if I were alone, I would go. What do you want to do?"

The tables had turned, and we again faced a decision regarding the wind. I knew that Chip had spent months with instructors learning to handle the unique behavior of tail-wheel aircraft under unfavorable conditions. I knew I was in good hands.

I remembered his words the day before and replied, "It's your call."

Moments later, we were climbing into the clear sky. I thought of Crazy Horse and his quest for a vision in the sacred Black Hills. When his great vision came to him, he knew that he would have to help his people wage a war that he did not wish to fight and could not be won, but that his courage — not his victory — would serve his people in the coming years of darkness. He also understood that he would never die by a white man's bullets. Thereafter, he rode fearlessly into battle, often returning into perilous situations to assist a wounded companion. No matter how hard they tried, the soldiers could never touch him with their bullets. Crazy Horse's courage was tempered by the knowledge that he would die at the hands of one of his own people. But this conferred an immunity from fear when it came to fighting the soldiers — a courageousness that has remained legendary among his people.

As we climbed through the lower clouds, it occurred to me that if I could be certain that death awaited me by some other means than crashing in a plane, this experience would be a pure delight. But no such guarantee was in the offing, nor is it ever for most of us. So I quietly repeated Crazy Horse's war cry — *Hoka hey!* It is a good day to die — and I surrendered to the moment.

We climbed to about 5000 feet and turned toward the sun. A silver ribbon of light appeared on the horizon: It was the sun's reflection in the Laguna Madre. My heart leapt, and I wanted so much to see my home waters from above. But today, we would not go there, for Chip was concerned about the rising wind. After circling over the Rio Grande River to the south and our childhood home a few miles to the east, we returned to the airport, made a complete circle of the field, and went in for a smooth landing.

I enjoyed the flight and found myself much less anxious than I usually am aboard a commercial jet. This was working, I realized, to qualm my lifelong fear of flying. But I also knew that I would not be finished until I had gone up for more than sightseeing. I wanted him to take it all the way and to do what the plane was designed to do — barrel rolls, aileron rolls, and loops. And then, perhaps, the greater portion of my fear — rooted in various memories of earlier times — would be gone for good, allowing me to live with less fear than before...and, perhaps, to catch the quarry that had thus far eluded me.

Almost 50 years after Jack's father sent me running for home in terror, Chip and Jack are still good friends. But Jack, for all of his humor and backslapping antics, seems a bit out of touch with himself. And further, until recently, he was unable to catch a single fish in five consecutive trips to the Laguna Madre.

During my stay on the water, Jack came down to South Texas on business, so he, Chip, and Spencer joined me one morning on the water. Chip took Jack out in his boat, and Spencer joined me in the Shoal Cat. Chip and Jack went north along the channel toward Port Mansfield, and Spencer and I stopped at Woody's Hole again. There we discovered that the reds were feeding in numbers just inside Woody's Hole and out into Payton's Bay. So we promptly got on the radio and called them to join us. Minutes later, Chip barreled through the skinny water separating the channel from Woody's Hole and came off plane 50 yards from where I stood. He and Jack piled out of the boat and headed our way. Within ten minutes, the four of us were standing side by side along the spoil bank on the south side of Woody's

Hole, near the place where Ryan had vomited his Cheerios just a few days before.

Statistically, the chances of each of us catching fish should have been about equal, for we were no more than 100 feet apart, spread out into Payton's Bay. Jack stood to my left, and then Spencer and Chip were just beyond JacKathy In little more than a half hour, I landed five redfish, using a small pink bendbacKathy It was a cloudless day — perfect for sight casting — and the reds were eager to take a fly. As a rule, they were not tailing, just cruising in pods of two or three, moving toward Woody's Hole with the outgoing tide. Chip and Spencer caught several, too, but Jack came up fishless once again. At one point, while I was fighting a nice red, I turned and encouraged Jack to get his lure in the water pronto! He just stood there, closer to the bank than the rest of us, fiddling with his lure. He seemed unmotivated and unsure of what to do.

Later, as we crawled aboard Chip's boat to have a soda before heading back, Jack sniffed the air and grimaced. "What's that smell?!" Remembering my exchange with Ryan, I answered, "That's the Laguna Madre. It's the height and the depth of her gift to us." He just looked at me like I was crazy. "Smells like *gugatha*[23] to me," he said, and then he laughed. I said nothing more, but I believed that his reaction accounted, in part, for his failure to catch fish.

Jack's response was inevitable, I am sure. Growing up in a hostile environment will drive anyone away from their own nature. It was how he'd survived, and it was how I had survived the various setbacks in my life. I was impressed by the irony of how his father — the perpetrator of his childhood wounds — had gone on to become healed by these smelly waters. He had left his son afflicted with wounds from an earlier time, and Jack remained unaware that the earthly smell around him signified the presence of a Mother's touch.

Several years ago, a few of the older men in town began gathering at the local hotel restaurant for afternoon coffee. Dad and Jack's

---

[23] Slang for feces

father Dale were the mainstays of this informal fraternity. The men took turns paying for the coffee, but for some reason on that fateful day, Dale picked up the check when it wasn't his turn.

Dad said, "Dale, it's not your turn to pay," to which Dale replied with a smile, "Spooky, it's my money and I can spend it any damn way I please!"

Then they went outside, and Dad saw that Dale had driven his new pickup to the restaurant and had backed it into the parking place.

Needling him further, Dad said, "Dale, when are you going to learn how to park that truck?"

Jack's dad laughed again, and said, "Spooky, it's my truck, and I will park it any damn way I please!" An hour or two later, Dale died at home of a heart attack while reading the paper.

A few months later, Jack returned to South Texas on a business trip. It was January, but it felt like summer. So my brother, who usually waits until March to begin fishing in earnest, took Jack out for another shot at redfish and trout.

Drifting down Dunkin's Channel, Jack had a new experience. Chip caught one fish, but Jack caught two big trout and a nice red. He had broken the spell on the heels of his father's death. If his father's sins had been visited upon him, then perhaps his father's healing had finally come upon him, too.

It is easy for me to imagine that Dale himself would have wanted it that way. Perhaps he returned in spirit that day to the waters that gave him life to oversee the beginning of his son's release from the past, as well.

Due to the chronic summer winds, and long days on the water, Chip and I had been unable to find time to fly again. In the mean time, he had fly fished with Kathy and me only once. Frustrated by a complete lack of success, he asked me after only a hour of fishing if he'd done enough yet. I said that I would leave that up to him. Without further discussion, he put the fly rod away, obviously believing that he'd discharged his part of our agreement. I was a little disappointed by how quickly he had reclaimed the status quo. As for myself, I knew that the first flight had been a good start, but that I needed to take it further. As my journey approached its end and another flying opportunity seemed remote, I gave up the idea of resolving my fears aloft in a more complete way.

But then, before the end of my trip, Chip surprised me by calling me one morning at 7:00 a.m. He had left that morning for the ranch, but he stopped at the airport and checked the forecast. The conditions were so good that he just had to go flying.

"Do you want to fly?" he asked. I felt immensely grateful for my brother's spontaneous offer. I said "Yes!" and jumped in my car.

When I arrived, Chip was already up with Spencer. So I waited nervously on the ground for them to return. Feeling nature's call, I went around the back of the hangar to the unofficial (and only) urinal and relieved myself against the hangar wall. As I stood there, I heard the little plane's engine overhead. Chip was coming to collect me. And at that moment, I noticed that an insect clung to the metal wall of the hangar just a foot in front of my eyes. I could hardly believe what I was seeing. It was, of all things, a blue-winged olive — a mayfly that I'd never seen in South Texas, even though I had collected insects for a good part of my adolescence. Having studied the stages of their emergence, I could see that the mayfly was incomplete in its metamorphosis. Its blue-gray wings told me that it was a "dun," not an egg-laying "spinner." Within a couple of days, I knew that he would shed his transitional body and then die mating over some nearby waters from which he had recently emerged.

I felt in that precious moment that God was conspiring with Nature to say, "You are ephemeral — destined to live only briefly before returning to the waters of life. So live now!" I took heart at this simple miracle, and I ran to meet Chip as he taxied up to the hangar to take me for the ride of my life.

Some seeds are slow to germinate, but in the summer of 2004, Chip and and Spencer took up fly fishing on the Lower Laguna Madre. Chip eventually sold his plane after suffering a bout of vertigo, and gave up flying altogether. While I am no longer afforded the privilege of flying with him, my fear of flying disappeared completely on the heels of our experiment in the summer of 1997.

Thursday, August 8, 2002, late afternoon
Arroyo City, Texas

I Obtain the Right Treatment

I accompanied Kathy and our client out on the bay, which I soon discovered was a serious mistake. I could barely stand the sensation of putting my foot down. So I kept my foot propped up as much as I could and guided Kathy in her search for fish. While I had experienced an emotional breakthrough the previous night, it became clear that I needed to return to the doctor. It had been six days since the stingray attack and I still was not getting any better.

As soon as we docked the boat I disappeared without saying a word to Kathy. I emerged from the house a little while later as she cleaned and gassed the boat, announcing that I was going back to the clinic. As I expected, her face evidenced her alarm.

When I took off the pus-soaked sock that I'd been using as a bandage, Ms. Dodson blanched.

"This is not good!" she exclaimed. She left the room abruptly, and a few minutes later I heard her say to the nurse through the closed door, "I should have changed his medication on Monday!" She returned with an open diagnostic manual turned to "Vibrio vulnificus" and began to devise a concerted plan of treatment.

It was late in the game for getting the proper treatment, but apparently not too late. She switched oral medications, prescribing Doxycycline, and gave me the first of two more powerful injections of Rocephin, which I later discovered was part of the recommended treatment regimen for vibrio vulnificus.

By Saturday morning, the infection was beginning to subside. It was only then that I was willing to see how close to death I had come. On Sunday, while Kathy was guiding, I went on the internet and researched Vibrio vulnificus. *What I learned made me realize that I was, indeed, fortunate to be alive, and that I couldn't have done more to undermine my recovery if I'd planned it.*

According to the Center for Disease Control, about half of those who develop bloodstream infections — characterized by the fevers and skin lesions that developed in my case — eventually die. My attempts at self-medication combined with Ms. Dodson's failure to diagnose my condition, left me without adequate medical treatment for several days. And while our pharmacist friend was correct about Cipro, he was wrong about Augmentin. A doctor told me later, "It might have cured an earache, but not a monster like Vibrio vulnificus." In spite of all of the mistakes that were made, the single injection of Rocephin on Monday may have forestalled the disease's progress just enough to save my life.

When I considered all of the ways that my recovery was delayed, it was obvious that on some level, the ordeal had been orchestrated. After all, I continued to fish when I should have come in, I failed to get medical attention on the day of the injury, and I obtained the wrong medication through Kathy's well-meaning efforts. And then, I chose a health care provider who was unaware of Vibrio vulnificus — a bacterium that can be lethal if not treated immediately.

However, the disease turned out to be a messenger of truth. By pushing me to the edge of a precipice, the illness forced me to find my way through my unacknowledged grief to the beginning of a new life.

12

The Manger

Arroyo City, Texas — mid-August 1997

"Oh night thou was my guide
A night more loving than the rising sun
A night that joined the lover to the beloved one
Transforming each of them into the other" [24]
St. John of the Cross

When I was a child in South Texas, Dad would take Chip and me out of school for two weeks every fall to go hunting in Choctaw County in southwest Alabama. Understandably, our principals expressed concern about the length of my absence, but when they called the superintendent for guidance on the matter, Mr. Fitzgerald — who often hunted and fished with my father — told them to let us go, saying simply, "They will learn more there than they will learn here."

Dad grew up on a small family farm near the Tombigbee River and hunted — more for sustenance than for pleasure — along the river for squirrels and deer during his childhood years. During our two-week visit, we'd hunt squirrels every day with my uncles Moody and Jake and then visit other relatives in the evenings. It was a glorious, innocent time, when the darker side of people, and the infirmities and addictions that would eventually claim them, were still largely unknown to me.

---

[24] *Loreena McKennit: The Mask and the Mirror.* 1994. New York: Quinlan Road Limited.

179

My grandfather was a game warden who had permission to hunt a low-lying area near the Tombigbee called the White Swamp. We left in the dark each morning and headed east toward the Tombigbee. Leaving the highway, we pursued a torturous trail through cultivated fields, pine and hardwood thickets, and second-growth meadows covered with briars and fire-ant hills the size of a car. An ordinary vehicle could never have made the trip, but my uncle Moody's 4-wheel-drive Ford pickup had a raised chassis to cope with the mud, and it was outfitted with a monstrous winch that could pull the truck across shallow creeks that flowed through the low-lying areas. It took over an hour just to go a few miles, and I often dozed against my father's shoulder, even though the truck felt like a roller coaster that had jumped its rail.

It was terribly cold and moist there in the morning. My feet would quickly become numb, and I would usually cry. My brother would make fun of me, but my dad would carry me as much as he could until the sun had warmed the thick carpet of rotting leaves. We hunted with squirrel dogs, and so, fortunately, we were always on the move. The dogs — a motley bunch distinguished by performance rather than breeding — would range ahead of us, checking each tree trunk for the fresh scent of squirrels.

In the midst of all of this activity, I can recall feeling very much alone. It was as if there was somewhere else I needed to be, some place where I would feel more secure and at home. I sometimes wished I was back at my grandfather's house, where there was always a fire in the hearth on cold autumn mornings. But even after I grew up, the feeling would settle over me like a ground fog, blurring the edges of the present and casting a chill over pleasurable activities of all kinds. For instance, on one occasion when I was 19, I was on a remote peninsula on the west coast of Mexico, fishing and skin diving with my buddies Roger and Mike. We'd been there almost two weeks, and we planned to stay three more days before making the long drive back across the Sierra Madres. But the old feeling came over me, and within an hour, we were packing for the 1000-mile trip. On another occasion, I was spending time alone at my log cabin in the Virginia Blue Ridge. I had planned to stay another day and to fly fish for brookies in one of my favorite headwater streams, Big Mary's CreeKathy But again the old feeling crept over me, and within a few minutes, I was heading back to Tidewater. After arriving home, as if emerging from a spell, I wondered why I had hurried bacKathy

It wasn't home that called to me, of course, because there's no lasting security to be found there or anywhere for that matter. The yearning was for a deeper connection that cannot be found by simply surrounding oneself with the familiar. It had come upon me at inopportune times and had disrupted my life sufficiently that I knew that someday it would have to be dealt with. Not surprisingly, the opportunity arose during my retreat, and it came through a subtle development in my relationship with the Laguna Madre.

Toward the end of our stay, Kathy and I began to notice that our rapport with Nature was increasing to the point where birds and animals exhibited little fear in our presence.

One morning, while I fished with Chip, Kathy carried out her daily spiritual practice — meditating for an hour just after her morning coffee. Near the end of the hour, she was aroused by an airy, screeching call just outside the window that she could not readily identify. She slowly opened the door and looked up into the tree. Only 20 feet away were two Harris's hawks, looking down at her with fearless interest. Although we sometimes spotted Harris's hawks on our side of the Arroyo, they were usually chasing prey and would return to the far side as soon as they had made their kill. Knowing that the hawk's appearance was extraordinary, Kathy quietly acknowledged the predator and then went back inside.

On another occasion, Kathy and I had been wading north of Dunkin's Channel in Rattlesnake Bay. We had already caught several redfish, and we were totally absorbed in the experience of sight casting to tailing and cruising reds. We had gone so far that we could barely see the boat behind us, but the long walk back did not deter us from forging ahead.

At one point, I saw a red approaching. Given the direction of the wind, I had to make a backhanded cast to him. I was lucky, for my cast placed the weedless bendback just in front of him, on the edge of a bank of grass. He rushed forward and inhaled the fly. As he made his first run, however, he pulled the line right through the thick grass. The leader picked up tufts of grass, putting a bend in the line and making it difficult for me to maintain a steady tension. From past experience, I knew I would probably lose him at any moment.

Then, about a hundred yards away, I saw a great blue heron take off and fly toward me. Expecting him to fly by, I was startled when he landed next to the redfish, about 30 feet from me. I watched spellbound as the heron walked beside the redfish, looking down at it and at my line. Wherever the redfish swam, the heron followed. Kathy saw what was happening and waded over to where I stood. We watched this drama together, not knowing what would happen next.

Then the heron bent over and began plucking the grass off my line! He removed a couple of small bunches, then stood up as the struggling redfish dragged the line under his legs. For a moment he straddled the line and then lifted off the water and flew away. A few minutes later, I landed the redfish and let him go.

Shortly afterward, I was fishing late one night on the lighted dock below the cottage. While casting to rising speckled trout, I noticed a blue heron sitting on the dock next door, watching me warily. It wasn't unusual to see an assortment of herons and egrets on nearby docks and pilings, so I soon forgot that the heron was there. A few minutes later, I hooked a foot-long trout and lifted it gently onto the dock, planning to remove the fly and to release the fish as quickly as possible. However, as I stepped toward the flopping fish, I noticed a movement out of the corner of my eye that made me hesitate. I looked up and saw the blue heron only 10 feet away, coming in for a landing. As I stepped back in surprise, he landed on the dock five feet from me, seized the fish without a moment's hesitation, and immediately took off across the water. Realizing that the fly was still in the fish's mouth, I grabbed my rod just in time. As the line tightened, the blue heron did a half-gainer and collapsed into the water. Meanwhile, the fish came out of its mouth, so I reeled it back in. Looking even more indignant than they usually do, the heron flew onto the neighbor's dock and stood there without moving, eyeing the fish — or me — with murderous intensity. Believing the fish to be injured by now, I removed the fly and laid it on the dock as an offering. The heron stared at the flopping fish, but would not come forward to claim the prize. So I released the trout, hoping that it would somehow survive the ordeal of having been captured twice in a span of moments.

A few days after this incident, I was fishing on the dock again and caught another small trout. As I lifted it out of the water, it dangled in midair as I tried unsuccessfully to grab it. Apparently, the sight of the dangling trout was too much for a nearby blue heron, because one suddenly appeared, wings outstretched, only a few feet away. I waved my arms and yelled, and it turned off at the last minute. I'm not sure what would have happened if the heron had kept on coming.

While I have since related these stories far and wide, I have heard of only one instance of a blue heron trying to take a fisherman's catch. Looking back, it is clear we we re being acknowledged by the Laguna Madre's predators not as outsiders, but as members in a cast of characters vying for the same rewards.

These strange encounters coincided with a gradual shift in our perspective. It was as though our desire to catch fish was giving way to a willingness to enter into the heron's realm and the trout's habitat — to become a part of their world. But we differed from our *compadres* in one significant way: We felt the urge to give as well as to take.

We kept this to ourselves, because the impulse led us to engage in activities that few people would have understood. Instead of eating all of the ground beef that Dad brought to us one evening, we took some of it out to the mouth of the Arroyo where we had observed coyotes roaming the banks in search of food. We beached the boat and left the meat on the shoreline, as a lone coyote watched us hungrily from 50 yards away. We dropped pieces of squid in front of stingrays and watched them eagerly devour the morsels. We fed the raccoons, as well, that paraded single file, red eyes glowing, along the bank across the Arroyo. And we even left bits of food for the roaches that swarmed over the docks at night. Later on, we discovered that this practice of ritually feeding wild animals is well known in India by the word *ahimsa* — a word that means "nonviolence," and which is considered an expression of one's essential unity with all of creation.

Of course, we kept fishing each day, but the level of our participation in Nature exceeded anything I'd known before. Kathy's presence assisted me in slowing down and entering into this deeper relationship, for she had a feminine willingness to stop and to see what was really going on. Slowly, without planning it, we were becoming immersed in the waters of life, sensitive to things that we would ordinarily overlooKathy

This willingness to go deeper into the natural realm gave rise to a sudden impulse to fly fish at night under the full moon. Fisheries biologists agree that big trout only feed two hours out of every 24, and that during a full moon, they will often complete their feeding during the night. To test the hypothesis that big trout can be caught more easily at night during a full moon, I went out one morning two hours before sunrise, to cast my VIP poppers by the light of the setting moon. I felt drawn to a small, inconspicuous cove on the west side of Rattlesnake Island — a place that was out of the way and rarely fished. At the west end of Rattlesnake Island was a bluff that loomed over the cove like the Sphinx, framing the shallow lagoon with imposing arms of cactus, mesquite, and Spanish dagger.

On that first occasion, I asked Chip to go with me. Since he often awakens around four and has trouble going back to sleep, he agreed to accompany me on this trial run. Even though he left his house 50 miles inland around four, he had to drive an hour to the Arroyo, and so the eastern horizon was already glowing when we arrived at our destination.

We anchored the boat on the southern end of the cove. Chip waded the main body of Rattlesnake Lagoon, leaving the tiny cove for me. He started off with topwater lures on his spinning rod, while I opted to use a tiny popper. I waded slowly into the southern end of the cove and noticed that glass minnows were rippling through the shallows. An occasional blowup indicated that a few game fish were gorging themselves on the abundant bait. After wading 100 feet, I finally spotted the black tip of a cruising trout's tail, but when I presented my popper, it ignored the fly and proceeded to leave the cove. Apparently, we'd arrived on the tail end of an all-night affair.

A local fishing tournament was coming up, and while I'd never fished in a tournament, the idea intrigued me once I learned that the event had a separate fly fishing division. Since the tournament began at sundown, and continued through the next day, the schedule would accommodate my desire to fly fish for big trout at night. Hoping for some companionship on the water, I called Chip and floated an idea that I was pretty sure he would reject.

"Why don't we enter the tournament? We could go back to Rattlesnake and spend all night fishing for trout on top." I braced myself for an almost certain no, but he surprised me.

"Sounds good," he replied. "Let me talk to Spencer and give you a call."

Later that day, he called and said they'd be down the next evening at 8:00 with their boat. The plan was simple: to anchor in the two entrances to Rattlesnake Lagoon — an area within the greater Rattlesnake Bay behind Rattlesnake Island — and have the area to ourselves from sundown until we decided to leave the area the next day. Given the fact that Rattlesnake had been full of redfish and trout for weeks, it was a clear winning strategy.

The only caveat in our ambitious plans was a tropical storm that was heading north from the Yucatan. We'd already experienced some rain bands, and it was possible that the night would be a wet one.

I wasn't concerned, however, because these squalls rarely have much lightning associated with them.

Kathy opted to stay ashore, but she helped us prepare the food we would need for the overnight quest. After signing in with the tournament officials, we launched our two boats at the Adolph Thomae County Park and headed for Rattlesnake Lagoon. Outfitted with walkie talkies to coordinate our movements, we separated as we approached the lagoon. I waved farewell and circled the island from the south, as Chip headed directly for the northwest entrance.

It was after 8:30 p.m. when I arrived at the southern entrance. I parked in the middle of the opening, even though I planned to fish the

cove against Rattlesnake Island. Not only did I want to discourage casual boat traffic, but I wanted to approach the cove on foot, as quietly as I could. I've often made fun of myself by saying to my fishing partners, "I've been known to park a 'mite fer piece' from the fishing hole." Indeed, I always err in the direction of leaving the prime water unmolested by the boat prop and attendant noise. But consequently, I have often walked long distances only to find the "fishing hole" devoid of life.

I tried to raise Chip and Spencer on the walkie talkie only to find that they were out of range. Since we had a clear plan, however, I wasn't concerned by our inability to communicate, because there would be plenty of time for that in the morning. I was more interested in fly fishing a bit before darKathy Even though the tournament began at nine, I wanted to fish so badly that I was willing to risk catching — and having to release — the big one before the tournament began.

I walked along the west edge of the lagoon, which was merely a bar between the lagoon and a shallow flat that extended westward to the shoreline of Atascosa Refuge, a mile away. During the high tides of spring and fall, the reds and trout will venture onto the shallower flat. But it was summer, and the fish would be holding in the lagoon itself.

I cast my popper into water that was about 15 inches deep. I looked at my watch and saw that it was a little before 9:00. A jet ascended 25 miles to the west, making no noise at all and reflecting the sunlight off its wings. Glowing as it did, it looked like a featureless ball of light gently turning towards me, framed by violet and canteloupe-colored clouds that shone with the spectral highlights of high-level ice crystals. As I stripped my topwater mindlessly, the sky seemed a harbinger of good things to come, and I was immensely happy for no other reason. About that time, a fish hit my fly and missed. It did not hit again, which relieved me of the moral burden of a fish in hand only minutes before the tournament would officially begin.

I went back to the boat, climbed up on my poling platform and sat dangling my legs and eating my favorite on-the-water snack — pretzels with Gatorade. Meanwhile, I looked toward the cove in the waning light and made mental notes of the approach I would take. Having forgotten about Chip and Spencer, I was startled by the sound of a boat approaching. Chip brought the Kenner off of plane and idled up to me, looking a bit sheepish.

"What's up?" I asked.

"I can't believe it, but I forgot our rain jackets, and there's a storm brewing," Chip said, as he pointed to a buildup that was still catching the setting sun's last rays. "And...I'm not really sure what we're doing out here," he added.

So much was conveyed in his words. I started to remind him of why we were there — to find the big trout under the full moon — but then I realized it was pointless. I was happy doing what I was doing, and it really didn't matter to me if he went in.

"I think we're going to go back in and come back in the morning," he said. "But we don't have a Q-beam, and I'm afraid we could hit something without a light."

"You can take mine," I said. I opened the dry storage compartment where I kept the searchlight.

"Are you sure you want to stay out here?" he asked, obviously feeling a little uncomfortable to be abandoning the plan we'd made and taking my only light.

"I want to stay." I pulled out the light and handed it to him. "I'll be here in the morning or fishing over near the White Bucket." I referred to the hot spot a half-mile to the north that had produced so well for us in years past.

By the time they'd attached the Q-beam to the boat's battery, it was dark, so Chip and Spencer faced a trip back to the mouth of the Arroyo with only the Q-beam to guide them. Saying goodbye, they turned the boat around and began to head across Rattlesnake Bay at a slow pace. Later on, they told me that they ran smack into the storm near the mouth of the Arroyo, and that they were completely soaked by the time they arrived back at the cottage.

I was oddly relieved that they had gone and felt immensely free. Meanwhile, the light in the west faded from purple to black, and the night became complete. I turned my stern light on and got my gear ready. I pocketed a tiny flashlight, which would assist me later in changing my flies in the dark, and put a small box of flies and some extra tippet in my waist pacKathy I turned off the light, so that my eyes would become adjusted to the dark, and downed some more pretzels and Gatorade. Then I slipped over the side into the shallow, dark water.

The spent storm cloud to the east glowed with a dull whiteness, revealing that the moon had just risen above the horizon. It would be an hour or more, I concluded, before the full moon would emerge from behind the feathery anvilhead. But in the meantime, the diffuse light would provide all I needed to discern the rough outlines of the cove.

I took a few steps toward the cove and let some line out. Just as I began false casting the popper, I was startled to see a whitish green light under the surface of the water sweeping ahead of me. I almost cried out and looked back over my shoulder, certain that someone had suddenly shined a searchlight into the water. But no one was there. Unsettled by the interruption, I looked around and tried to figured out what had made the light. Taking another step, I was again startled by several lights shooting through the water away from me. Still reeling from the anomaly, I looked down only to see that the water around my legs was on fire with a surreal greenish-white light. It was phosphorescent plankton! I was stunned, having never seen this phenomenon in the shallow flats of the Lower Laguna, but then again, I had only fished at night once before. As I moved forward, I realized that the shooting lights were fish fleeing my presence and leaving phosphorescent trails in their wakes. I laughed in relief.

I waded as quietly as possible along the bank of Rattlesnake Island toward the back of the cove. Unable to see very much at all, I stopped and listened, hoping to hear the sounds of feeding gamefish. At first, all I could hear was something resembling a gurgling mountain stream. As I listened more carefully, I realized that the water was teeming with glass minnows that were rippling through the shallow water, making an almost constant tinkling sound.

I felt as though I was immersed in a single organism comprised of water, fish, moon, and sky. My awareness began to shift away from being a fisherman to a becoming a part of this great interconnected being.

This feeling was nothing new and had attached itself to the *ahimsa* practice and to our daily meditations, as well. The origins of this shift in my relationship to Nature and to life as a whole had begun almost two years earlier.

Before Kathy and I had met, I had been involved with a woman who I loved very much. Our plans were to be married once her divorce was finalized. However, our relationship was not strong enough to withstand the deep emotional patterns that we each carried forward from the past. We did not belong together, and I was only beginning to realize it. During one of our arguments, I fled the house and drove to my office to stay the night. I stuffed clean underwear and my toothbrush in the file cabinet with my client records, and then I laid down on the sofa in my clothes. I felt so utterly alone, and I recalled the eerie, displaced feeling I'd experienced while hunting with my father in the White Swamp along the Tombigbee River of southwest Alabama: I longed to be somewhere else, but I did not know where.

As I fell asleep on the sofa, I knew deep down that it was only a matter of time before the relationship was over. I was sad, but mainly I was frightened that I was in a relationship that was so intense and complex that its dissolution would bring immense pain and chaos to my life again, only two years after leaving my marriage.

Hours later, I was awakened by the sound of rushing wind. Like so many times before, it took complete hold of me and awakened a profound sense of ecstasy and love. Having experienced this phenomenon many times already, it was like an old friend coming to visit.

I tried to let go, but it's never easy, because it doesn't let you keep anything back for yourself. C. S. Lewis once said that most of us are like the good man who pays his taxes and hopes that there will be something left for him. Lewis says, "With Christ, it's much simpler than that: He wants it all." If there's one thing I've learned, there can be absolutely no holding back when it comes to an encounter with the Divine.

I felt a Person behind the energy, but I saw no one. As it subsided, I sat up and meditated, happy that God would reach out to me at such a time. As I entered a deep peace that often comes on the heels of ecstasy, I beheld a sudden clear vision of a medium blue cloth. As I marveled at its beauty, I could see every thread sharply defined. And then it was gone.

Since I had been working on a book about visions of Mary, the mother of Jesus[25], I associated the blue cloth with Mary's mantle, which is often experienced by visionaries as a medium blue color. In the days that followed, in spite of the emotional turmoil of an unraveling relationship, the memory of the blue cloth and its fine threads served to remind me that I was overshadowed by a love and a deep connectedness that would see me through this life crisis.

Not long after that comforting vision, I began to experience a related phenomenon that continues to this day. Whenever I meditate and manage to become completely absorbed in the experience, there are brief moments when I lose my awareness of who I am and where I am. In those precious moments of communion, parallel lines often appear — "burned" into my visual field like the afterimage of a bright light. These lines may appear as several parallel lines, and at other times as a screen, or a grid, that remains visible for a few seconds. And on still other occasions, it manifests as a beautiful cloth.

After meeting Kathy, and beginning to meditate together each morning, she, too, began to experience what we came to call "the lines" in almost every deep meditation. These common visions were unprecedented in my years of spiritual practice. Gradually, the lines appeared concurrently with brief visions of close friends, family members, or therapy clients, who would often appear in or behind the matrix of lines. From what we could gather later, the visions are always symbolic of the true state of affairs in the other person's life. As we contemplated the meaning of the lines and the attendant visions, we realized that we were becoming profoundly interwoven with each other and with other souls, and that the Mother's mantle in my initial vision signified a growing capacity to enter into communion with all of life. This emerging sense of oneness had a secondary effect on me, related to my childhood sense of being far from where I needed to be. I began to feel at home wherever I was, seamlessly connected to the places I visited and to the persons and animals who lived there.

---

[25] Sparrow, G. S. 1997. *Blessed Among Women: Encounters with Mary and Her Message.* New York: Harmony.

And so, as I ventured into the darkness, wading in waters rippling with life, I felt none of the insecurity that had plagued me as a child. I was grateful to be there, and I looked forward with every step to the discovery that awaited me.

As I waded more deeply into the cove, the popping sounds of feeding trout greeted me, so I began to cast blindly into the dark water. My eyes became so accustomed to the low light of the cloud-shrouded moon that I began to see the surface disturbances of the feeding fish. I was rewarded by what seemed to be two strikes, but the fish missed the fly and did not return for a second looKathy

I made it about half way across the lagoon, before I circled back toward to the boat to inspect my gear and have a snacKathy It was almost midnight when the moon emerged from behind the clouds. Having become accustomed to the diffuse light, the exposed orb was, at first, unpleasantly bright. Fortified by a sandwich that Kathy had made for me, I set out for a longer wade that would take me far from the boat and more deeply into the night.

Casting continuously, I entered into a sense of timelessness. Undistracted by other sights and sounds, I began to look up and contemplate the stars as my line zipped overhead, and the tiny popper sent its invitation into the night.

My reverie was interrupted by the sight of a light in the northern sky. Like a bright star, it shone through the thin clouds, waxing and waning with the thickness of the veil. But when it finally emerged into the open blackness, it continued to pulsate as it moved slowly toward the horizon, bypassing the familiar constellations and planets. It was, I realized, a satellite that was tumbling end over end in its journey toward the edge of the world.

A wind came from behind me, announcing an approaching storm. The moonlight revealed a squall line, coming from the south that would reach me in only minutes. It was too late to return to the boat, so I waded to the shoreline of Rattlesnake Island and sat down on the grassy banKathy Putting my hood on, and laying my rod on the grass, I bowed my head in wait.

Again, I felt no urge to flee, for there was no better place to be. The wind-blown rain raked across the estuary, disturbing the mirror-like sheen of the water. There was no lightning, thankfully, so I was free to enjoy the sense of full immersion that the warm rain and wind brought to me.

Minutes later, it had moved to the north, so I resumed my wade in that direction until I reached the shoreline of Horsehead Island. I sat for a while on the bank and nibbled on a bar that I'd tucked into my pocket. The boat was a half mile to the south, shining brightly under the moon's full gaze. Soon I got up and headed back, realizing that while the effort had failed to reap a trophy trout, it had brought me a sense of deep contentment.

When I crawled back onto the boat, it was almost 4:00 a.m., and I was dead tired. Using my seat cushion as a pillow, I laid down on the front deck of the Shoal Cat, pulled my hood down over my face, and began to doze off. Another light shower swept through, but I just pulled the hood down lower and let the water pour onto the decKathy Then, I finally fell asleep.

Some time later, I had a dream. I was walking up to a small rustic building out in the middle of an open plain. I opened the door to enter, and a brilliant golden light greeted me. I went inside, and the light grew brighter and brighter, until the features of the room disappeared in the glow. I suddenly became aware that I was dreaming and began to wonder where I was. As I pondered the question, the answer was finally given as two words — burned into my mind just as the lines had been etched over and over again in my deepest meditations:

The Manger.

And then I passed out of the dream into sleep and was interrupted some time later by the sound of an outboard motor.

I opened my eyes and realized that it was daylight, and that Chip and Spencer were approaching. I got up slowly, aching from the short night on the unforgiving decKathy

"Did you do any good?" Spencer yelled.

"No. But I had a great time," I answered back, still reeling inwardly from the memory of the dream.

"We're going over to the White Bucket. Do you want to go with us?" Chip asked.

I told them I'd start fishing where I was and then head their way. Defying my weariness, I signed up for another mile-long round-trip wade. But I had grown to love this place and wanted to fish the cove again in the light of day. Hours later, after catching no fish, I waded up to Chip and Spencer only to learn that Spencer had already caught a 25-inch trout and Chip a 26-inch red, among other smaller fish. Fishing alongside them, I managed to catch a 23-inch red that I released, unwilling to kill such a modest fish just to make sure I'd have something to weigh in. Dead tired, my angling skills soon faltered under the stress of the day, and I gradually conceded that the tournament was over for me.

In spite of the outcome, I was deeply content. I could not begin to tell my brother and his son what had taken place. But I was sure that I would never again feel that I was too far from home — for home had become the ground I walked upon, and the waters in which I waded. I had found a place within me that would give rise to new life, perpetually, as I tumbled brightly, waxing and waning, toward the edge of this world.

The Light Returns

Two years after the vibrio vulnificus *infection, my ankle remains permanently altered. The skin is slightly darker than the surrounding flesh, and the scar tissue that encircles my ankle limits my range of movement. But I have my foot, and my life, and a renewed appreciation for the grace that can come in a wounding experience.*

Not long after I recovered from the infection, a momentous dream indicated that another form of healing had taken place.

In the dream, I was with an unknown woman. Both of us were afflicted with an incurable, fatal disease.

That night, we went to sleep in separate beds, only a few feet apart. In the middle of the night, I was overcome by a brilliant white light. I surrendered to it as fully as I could, aware that the resistance I've often felt during such encounters seemed, at last, nonexistent. I was also conscious that the Light was passing through me into the woman. As the Light came in pulsating waves of ecstasy, I heard a man's voice say, "Your mortal life is over."

When I awakened in the morning, both the woman and I had been healed of our illnesses, and I knew that we would remain together for all eternity.

13

The Way of Surrender

Arroyo City, Texas — mid-August 1997

*

> *"Beloved, gaze in thine own heart.*
> *The Holy tree is growing there."*
> William Butler Yeats

The last day dawned slightly cooler than it had been since I'd arrived in South Texas. Clouds to the south over the Gulf hinted of the tropical wave off the coast of Mexico, and there was a virtual absence of wind, a sure sign of something brewing. The day before, Kathy and I had decided to take the boat out of the water rather than squeezing in one last trip. We were both sad to see our time on the boat come to an end, but we needed some rest before we started the long drive back to Virginia.

As a compromise, I suggested that we drive along the bay road to Port Isabel, cross over the causeway to Padre Island, and then head up the island to fish one last time. There we would wade from the island into the east side of the Laguna Madre onto the "white sand," an area where the water is almost always crystal clear and the bottom firm and easily wadeable. We would fish near the place where I won the scout fishing tournament when I was 14. Ending up there would be like coming full circle.

Kathy voiced what was also on my mind. "Let's drive through the refuge once more, okay? I'll drive for you this time."

I readily agreed, knowing that the Laguna Atascosa National Wildlife Refuge had become sacred ground for both of us. I had grown

198

up and moved away from South Texas without ever visiting the place. Then, two weeks before Kathy arrived, my brother Chip suggested that we drive into the 45,000-acre refuge just before dark to look for deer.

I expected to see an unbroken expanse of thick, continuous virgin brush land bordering the Laguna Madre. I did not realize that the woods actually surrounded a huge inland lagoon — the namesake of the refuge. Just before dark, we ended up at an observation site called the Osprey OverlooKathy I got out of the car and was overwhelmed by what I saw: The setting sun was sinking into a water-filled crater in the middle of an expanse of prickly pear, Spanish dagger, and mesquite.

I went back the next day alone. I wondered how I had lived only 40 miles away and never knew such a place existed. It made me wonder what other beauty I overlooked each day.

Upon returning to the cottage that night, I placed a cutting of aromatic wildflowers next to Kathy's picture beside my bed and looked forward to taking her to the refuge once she arrived.

When Kathy visited the refuge for the first time — only two weeks before the end of my retreat — we arrived in time to watch the sun set majestically over the lagoon. She, too, was deeply moved by the unusual beauty of the lagoon and the surrounding area. While I had hoped she would like the area, I expected her — as a native of upstate New York — to find the South Texas brush country too stark for her tastes. But after fishing the Laguna Madre and roaming the Laguna Atascosa Refuge for a week, she told me that the entire area had touched her more profoundly than any place she'd ever been.

"I love this place," she said. "And I would come back here, even if I was alone."

I knew that she was referring obliquely to the indeterminate status of our relationship. Despite our love for each other, neither of us knew for sure if we would ever return to this place together.

I had come to the Laguna Madre, in part, to obtain a fresh perspective on my life. Outwardly, I was pretty much a success as a writer and a psychotherapist. But inwardly, I felt a deep weariness and did not know for sure if I could continue performing the duties that had previously defined me in the world. Kathy supported my quest for spiritual renewal from the first moment that she learned of my calling to return to my home waters. She knew that if we were ever to be together, it would be on the far side of my journey home.

Just before I left for Texas, I dreamed that I was with the woman I loved. We had both been to heaven before, and we both wanted to return; but we knew that we had to find our way homeward along different paths. She could return by going inward — by meditating until the gates of her heart opened and she found herself back in paradise. However, I could only find my way back by embarking on a solitary journey through a vast wooded region. I needed a map and was finally able to obtain one with enough detail to assist me on each leg of my journey. I was excited, thinking that both of us would find the way to our true home. I intended to make it to heaven before she did and to greet her when she arrived.

Although the unknown woman in my dream was clearly my *anima* — not an actual woman — Kathy and I faced the same dilemma that the woman in the dream and I faced: Our lifelong goals were clearly congruent, but we were not yet sure that we could pursue them together.

We approached our time on the Laguna Madre with this sobering thought in the background, but our time on the water brought us closer than ever before. Our spiritual and emotional rapport deepened as we meditated together, fished under the full moon, stalked tailing redfish under a midday sun, and fed hamburger to the coyotes. Toward the end of the trip, we realized that, ultimately, it did not really matter if we lived together for the rest of our lives or not; for, regardless, we were building a legacy of shared sacred experiences that would endure forever.

As we drove the 17 miles to the entrance to the refuge, I reflected back on the past month and, in particular, on the last few days with Kathy. With her as a companion, I had finally settled into the experience of just being in Nature. Seeing the deer and the hawks in the refuge had become as precious as catching trout in the Laguna Madre. I felt tears welling up as I recalled the times we'd spent on the water and in the refuge and the inexplicable phenomena that we had witnessed together. I was thinking, in particular, about the night we'd spent on the bay just two days before.

After our aborted night on the bay only 10 days earlier, I felt we needed to try spending the night on the water again before our time ran out. So, two days before we were scheduled to leave, we headed out at 11:00 p.m., navigating by the moonlight alone. The sky was almost cloudless, and the wind had died entirely. The unbroken surface of the bay was like another sky in which all the stars and a separate moon were replicated with an exacting precision. Only the occasional mullet jumping broke the illusion that heaven and earth were one and the same.

We turned north at the mouth of the Arroyo toward Woody's Hole, a place where the big trout often gather on the outgoing tide. I pulled over onto the edge of the flats and anchored. As I put my booties on, I noticed that Kathy was sitting quietly, looking at the stars.

"Look at that!" She suddenly pointed at the sky with awe in her voice. Looking up, I caught the tail end of a bright green light passing overhead. It left a smoky trail against the night sky.

"Wow, I wonder what that was!" I exclaimed. "Maybe space debris reentering the atmosphere."

But then it happened again. A greenish light streaked overhead, leaving the same smoking signature.

"I don't know anything about this," I said. "Maybe it's a meteor shower, but I've never seen them in chartreuse!"

The sound of a dolphin breathing interrupted our speculations. They were coming within a few feet of the boat, and we could see their dark shapes above the silvery surface. And then, I heard what I'd hoped to hear — the popping sounds of trout feeding along the channel.

"I'm going wading. Care to join me?" I asked.

"No, thanks," Kathy replied. "I think I'll stay and cast from the boat. As I recall, the stingrays are thick here, aren't they?" she asked.

"As fleas," I said. "But I'll be careful."

I waded 50 feet to the north, and began casting a topwater over the edge of the channel and back to my left onto the flat, as well. Almost immediately, I heard the sound of a fish striking and saw the dark circle of her rise, so I struck on the assumption that the fish had taken my fly. I felt resistance and lifted my rod to fight the first of numerous trout and ladyfish that would take my fly over the next three hours. For a while, I gave Kathy a play-by-play update, but soon she fell silent, so I left her alone. Having caught nothing, she had obviously laid down and fallen asleep. Meanwhile, the recurrent sounds of fish feeding and dolphins breathing only a few feet away — and the never-ending stream of mysterious green lights passing overhead — seemed, by this time in our journey, far more than coincidental. It seemed like the beginning of a final show of support that had been there all along.

I released all of the fish that I could, but two 20-inch trout were bleeding too much to survive release. Using a small penlight that temporarily ruined my night vision whenever I would turn it on, I was able to string the two wounded fish. *Dad will be pleased*, I thought.

Around 3:00 a.m., the moon sank behind some clouds, and it was as though someone turned off a switch. The fish abruptly stopped hitting on top and would not, thereafter, take my fly. So, I waded back the boat and woke Kathy.

"Where do you want to sleep?" I asked.

"I was doing fine here," she laughed. "But I guess we should anchor away from the channel."

"How about the Mud Hole?" I suggested, since it was one of her favorite spots. "We can fish there at sunrise."

I could feel her smiling. "Sounds good to me," she said.

We headed back south and anchored in the mouth of the Mud Hole. I spread my sleeping bag over the front deck and used it as a cushion. The August night was far too warm for covers, and anyway I wanted nothing between myself and the sky. As usual, Kathy climbed inside her bag and zipped it up.

"I'm cold," she said.

"You're always cold," I reminded her.

As far as I know, there were no dreams of white light that night, but even if some great dream had come, I would probably have forgotten it upon awakening. For it could hardly have improved upon dolphins and trout and ladyfish feeding in the moonlight, and mysterious lights passing overhead.

The night had been enough.

The sun was still low on the horizon as we entered the refuge. It was the first time we had visited the place in the early morning, and I was hoping that we would see even more wildlife than we'd seen before. We had seen chachalacas, Harris's hawks, armadillos, deer, and many of the other animals indigenous to the area. We had even observed a rare Aplomado falcon that flew out over the open tidal plain on the occasion of our second visit to the refuge. But today I hoped that Kathy would get to see the elusive peccary, or javelina.

We drove slowly toward the edge of the Laguna Madre, across salt flats and through scattered thickets. It was hard to believe that the area once served as a target practice zone for pilots destined to see action during World War II. Somehow the land had absorbed and forgotten all of that violence. The only evidence that remained of the sound and fury were the bent and broken bullets that could be found scattered on the ground.

The chachalaca and their young chicks lined the road in the early morning light, and two bucks in velvet bounded off toward a thicket across a salt marsh. As we rounded a bend in a thickly wooded area, we finally came upon what we'd hoped to see — javelina standing in the road eating a piece of prickly pear. We stopped the car and watched as they turned the cactus over and over, eating it as if it didn't have two-inch thorns covering every square inch of its surface.

"You have been very fortunate," I said to Kathy for the hundredth time. She nodded. She knew that she had witnessed things that few people had ever seen.

As we drove further, we came upon a family of Harris's hawks sitting atop some tall mesquite trees. I suggested that we pull over so we could get a better looKathy The hawks seemed curious, and they watched us as we stopped and rolled down our windows. I sat looking at an immature, or "passage," male hawKathy

I held my palm to my mouth and made a noise that I'd made hundreds of time as a youth hunting in the woods along the Rio Grande River — the sound of a wounded rabbit. The young Harris's wheeled around in the tree and crouched to get a better look at the source of the sound. Then, to my amazement, he swooped down toward the car and passed just above my window as I let out a cry of surprise. Once again, I found it hard to comprehend why animals kept responding to us in such remarkable ways. It was as if the birds and the coyotes and the deer perceived us as one of them.

"You have been very fortunate," I repeated, not knowing what else to say. She smiled, and we both chuckled.

A few minutes later, we arrived at Stover's Point — a promontory above the Laguna Madre. Indians must have once considered this sacred ground, for it is the highest point within miles. The 360-degree view it afforded us of the bay and the surrounding area was spectacular. The rising sun bathed everything in a golden glow, including a single boat that was anchored just off the point. Two men and a woman were wading out in front of the boat, beside which a guide stood watching and waiting. One fly fisher refrained from casting as he waded, waiting for some sure sign to justify his efforts. The other two were casting blindly in the direction of their hopes. The woman waded out in front of the men and conveyed a graceful intensity that made me think of Kathy.

It felt strange to be there, looking down upon them. In essence, we were witnessing our own efforts over the past few days played out before us. Kathy and I still yearned to be out there, but we had chosen first to pay homage to the refuge before wading into the Laguna Madre one last time. I squinted my eyes against the morning sun, and I could see the guide standing beside his boat, training his binoculars on us.

The sight of the group fishing increased our desire to be on the water one last time. So we got back into the Rodeo and continued our drive along the bay and through the refuge. Driving a little faster than before, we said our silent goodbyes to the land and the wildlife around us.

Kathy asked me if I was disappointed that I hadn't caught a big trout on my fly rod. I said, no, that I was completely at peace with what had happened. I thought back on all that I'd learned about fishing and about myself, and all the opportunities that I'd been given to be in Nature and with those whom I loved. Somewhere along the way, I had surrendered the need to catch anything out there to make me happy. In its place, I had connected inwardly with everyone and everything that had graced my life in the last few weeks. Everything now fit perfectly into an emerging sense of completeness, including the frustrations that I'd encountered fly fishing for big trout.

"I don't need to catch a big trout," I said. "This — the entire experience — is what I came for. I know that now."

The roadrunners, rabbits, and chachalaca scurried ahead of us, leaving their tracks in the sandy road that led us onward. We passed through the refuge gate and headed toward Padre Island.

Kathy and I put the Rodeo in four-wheel drive several miles north of the town of South Padre Island and left the highway. After driving west across the sand to the edge of the Laguna Madre, we turned north and began looking for the wreckage of a plane that had gone down several years before. It was near there, Cecil had said, that schools of redfish might be found at high tide in water that was less than a foot deep.

We drove about as far as we could and reached a spot four miles directly east of where we'd fished for the last five days. The bottom was so firm and clean that we considered wading barefoot, but then we thought better of it. We realized that we might be facing a long walk back to the car on the hot sand.

After we had waded out a few yards, we could see the glint of the sun reflecting off the tails of feeding fish.

"Black drum," I announced. "You have to cast the fly close enough for them to see it. If you get it even an inch too close, they will spook and never look bacKathy Cast the fly about a foot in front of them, then jiggle it toward you and watch what they do. If you see them follow it, jiggle it ever so slightly and then let it sit in the sand. If you see them turn to one side, they have either picked up the fly or have lost interest — probably the latter. In either case, that's when you set the hooKathy Firmly and quickly!"

The morning was simply exquisite. The water was cool and gin-clear. The wind had increased by the time we arrived, but only enough to provide a cool breeze and send a ripple over the surface of the water. Small pods of drum could be seen everywhere, waving their tails in the air as they grubbed in the sand. We enjoyed a clear view of fish feeding all around us, even though they proved difficult to catch, as usual.

We separated after wading out about 200 yards from the shoreline and swept northward. We were still in only 15 inches of water, and it would remain at that depth for another half mile at least. I waded on the outside, while Kathy stayed closer to the shoreline. We weren't sure where we'd find the reds, but we hoped to increase our chances of locating them by spreading out. Outfitted with the walkie talkies, she and I quietly kept each other apprised of what was happening. We moved slowly. The drum were everywhere, and it was challenging to try to get one to take the fly.

I fiddled around, casting to every drum that came my way, and I finally caught one - a small two-pound fish. Kathy had never seen one close up, so she came over to look at it and to touch it before I let it go. Then, after making numerous attempts, she hooked a drum briefly, but it came off.

A bit later, I heard Kathy's voice on the walkie talkie. "A red!" she said excitedly.

I looked over and she was crouching low to the water, making a cast the north. "Missed him!" she said.

I thought I'd better get serious if I was going to catch a redfish, so I let out more line and began casting slightly off to my right, back toward the island — leaving the water directly ahead of me unmolested by my fly line. I stripped my fly without looking at it; meanwhile, I studied every inch of the water in front of me. I didn't really expect to catch a fish by blind casting, but I wanted to have enough line out to be able to cast immediately to any incoming fish that I spotted.

Suddenly, I saw a fish closing in from the north that was still about 90 feet away. I'd already seen a hundred drum approach from the same angle, but something told me that it wasn't a drum this time.

I lifted 50 feet of fly line out of the water, changed direction in midair, and double-hauled 70 feet of line downwind toward the rapidly approaching fish. I figured that if my cast was off the mark, I'd have time to pick up and try once or twice again before the fish saw me. But the first cast was right on the money — about four feet directly in front of the fish. I began stripping the fly toward me as it hit the water to imitate a fleeing bait fish, and the fish suddenly accelerated to intercept it. As it lunged forward, I knew that it had either taken the fly or missed it entirely.

Leaving my rod tip low to the water, I stripped and felt the firm response of a sizable fish. It was on! Just at that moment, its head came out of the water, and a large yellow mouth thrashed violently. A big trout had taken my fly! I cried out, but Kathy was already aware of what was happening.

"A trout, right? I see the yellow mouth!" She was thrilled by the sight of the fish breaking the water.

"Yeh, a pretty big one, too!" I shouted. I could hardly believe it. The trout was full of life and did not come in easily. After a good fight, the fish came close, and I saw that it was about five pounds. It was far from a world record, but it was a beautiful fish and the largest trout that I'd caught during my trip.

Before releasing her, I held her in the water and admired her beauty. Her silvery body was almost blinding in the sunlight, so I turned her slightly to see the sweep of iridescent rose along the lateral line and the constellation of spots for which she was so aptly named *cynoscion nebulosus*, or "starry nebulae." As she swam away, cloaked in the browns, blacks, and greens of her mottled back, she appeared as a slowly moving shadow against a canvas of white sand and became one of my fondest memories.

Shaking myself out of the spell that the fish had cast over me, I was stunned by the way things had happened. After a month of trying fruitlessly to catch big trout, a beautiful fish had come out of nowhere and taken my fly when I'd least expected it.

"I can't believe it!" I said. "I'd given up all hopes of catching a big trout, and then it happened!"

"That's why it happened, don't you think?" Kathy asked.

Of course, she was right. If I had never come to regard fly fishing as part of my spiritual journey, catching a big trout would have been far easier. But over the years, my fly fishing had come under the "rules" of spiritual practice. For better or worse, I knew there was no going back to a more innocent time when mere luck might have prevailed. Remembering the breakthroughs I had experienced in meditation and deep dreams, I recalled that only when I have surrendered completely has Spirit blessed me with its grace.

And so, it was to be expected: The big trout came to my fly only once I'd surrendered the need to have it.

Soon, it was time to go, so we waded the quarter mile back to the car. Looking back across the water, we could barely see Dunkin's house on the horizon, surrounded by the waters of the Laguna Madre. Beyond that familiar landmark lay the shallow channel and spoil banks where we'd finally located the huge trout near the end of our retreat. We took one last look and hugged each other on the sand before we dismantled our rods and packed our gear away.

On the way back, I looked at Kathy riding beside me, and I felt a deep affirmation of my love and respect for her. She had been there for me without losing her own way, and, in the course of about two weeks, she had embraced the Laguna Madre as her home waters. She had faced her fear of stingrays and had stalked, caught, and released big fish without my assistance.

As for myself, I was approaching an inner peace that transcended any contentment I'd ever known. When I thought of my family and my friends, I felt connected with each of them as never before. I felt Ryan with me in every waking moment. And Dad and I were closer than we'd ever been.

I then thought of a dream with Jesus that happened three years before.[26] In that brief experience, he asked me if I loved him. Of course, I said yes. Then he asked me if I loved Mary. Not sure what he meant, I nonetheless said, "Yes." Then he said, "Then you are my father and my brother."

These words have inspired me and confused me every day of my life since then.

I felt at the time that Jesus meant Mary, his mother. But as my retreat to the Laguna Madre came to an end, a magnificent dream came to me a few days before we left, and it showed me that loving Mary meant even more.

---

[26] Sparrow, G. S. 1995. *I Am with You Always: True Stories of Encounters with Jesus.* New York: Bantam.

In the dream, I became aware that a group of hunters, of which my stepfather and father were members, had come upon a Native American man in the woods. Thinking of him as no more than an animal, they had killed him and beheaded him, keeping his head as a trophy. I was horrified and convinced that the crime had to be reported. While most of the hunters expressed no remorse whatsoever, my father wore a pained, confused look about what they had done. As I talked to him about our need to take action, it was as if he slowly awakened from a deep sleep and finally acknowledged the truth. Then I called the authorities and told them what had happened.

As I hung up, I became aware that a cougar was making its way into deep South Texas — passing through the King Ranch, skirting the U.S. Border Patrol check point at the little town of Sarita, and moving into the area near the Mexican border where I had grown up. I was hopeful that it would thrive there.

Then, suddenly, I was aware that I was dreaming. I walked south through a meadow and looked up to see a beautiful, dew-covered red hibiscus hanging over my head. I took a few more steps and affirmed that when I looked up the next time, I would see the Holy Light. I lifted my eyes and beheld a huge orb of white light surrounded by a delicate, lattice-like corona that took up most of the sky. I knew that it was the Light of Christ.

Then an elderly woman approached from behind me. Her eyes told me that she loved me. I reached out, put my arm around her, and kissed her forehead, knowing that she was Mary, the mother of Jesus. We turned back toward the Light and saw that a second light had appeared to the left, slightly below the white orb. The new light was bluish-violet and — with delicate, hairlike filaments of light — resembled the blossom of a passionflower. I turned to Mary and said, "Is that your light?" She nodded.

I turned back and looked again, only to see that a third light had joined the other two. It appeared to the right, slightly below the white orb. It shone from the window of a tower whose base now stood only a few feet away from us.

"Whose light is that?" I asked.

Mary replied, "It's Mary Magdalene's light."

Then I said, "Do you want to go there?" Again she nodded, so we walked forward and began to climb the tower's circular stairs. Then I awakened.

My journey homeward meant so much more than catching fish. It meant reclaiming the primal spirit and depth of feeling that had been suppressed for most of my life. By remaining "severed from my body," I had remained half a man, incapable of truly loving a woman, whose emotional depth and intensity I had feared and disavowed in myself. Loving Mary also meant loving the Magadalene, whose love of Jesus apparently overshadowed whatever imperfections history has ascribed to her.

I looked around me, and I knew, in a larger sense, that Mary was the mother of these waters and that she held the refuge under her mantle. Her spirit infused the woman who had come to me in reverie to teach me about myself and had comforted the young Mexican prostitute whose sadness still haunted me. She abided, most imminently, in my companion who sat quietly beside me. She was also the heart and soul of me, residing in my strengths and in my weaknesses, too. She was the one who said yes to spirit and who conceived its fullness as a new life within her.

As I had loved this Being, and cared for her in her many guises, I was becoming "the unborn son" that was foretold in my coming-of-age dream. I was becoming the father, lover, friend, and son to the ones who had loved me throughout my brief sojourn in this place. I no longer felt as disconnected from the greater life within me. I was on my way home.

A poem by Whitman came to mind as we drove back to the highway, saying goodbye to the pelicans, gulls, and skimmers that lined the shore waiting for something to happen, we knew not what.

And you, O my Soul, where you stand,
Surrounded, surrounded, in measureless oceans of space,
Ceaselessly musing, venturing, throwing, — seeking the

> *spheres to connect them;*
> *Till the bridge you will need, be form'd — till the ductile*
>   *anchor hold;*
> *Till the gossamer thread you fling, catch somewhere,*
> *O my Soul.*[27]

Kathy and I sat quietly musing as we traveled across the miles of sand. When we finally pulled up onto the pavement and shifted out of four-wheel drive, I reached over and took her hand.

"Let's do this again, okay?" I said.

She leaned over and kissed me.

Fly fishing for trophy speckled trout poses a daunting challenge to even the most skilled angler. To succeed at catching them with any regularity, a fly fisher must exercise prodigious stealth, learn to see what others overlook, and wait patiently for opportunities to present themselves. Once he succeeds in merging seamlessly with the realm where big trout rule, he will discover that there is a palpable sense of magic that accompanies the quest. He may realize, as I did during my retreat, that the quest for the "starry nebulae" accurately mirrors a deeper desire for meaning and wholeness, and that as an unexpected consequence of angling for this "difficult" fish, he may discover something in himself that is not so elusive as it is waiting — and not so difficult as it is beautiful.

---

[27] Van Doren, M. 1945. *A Noiseless, Patient Spider,* in *The Portable Walt Whitman.* New York: Viking.

Appendix

My Favorite Big Trout Flies
and How to Tie Them

VIP Popper

Uses: This is an excellent attractor for big trout in low light conditions. I use it in the early morning, and under full moon along the edge of the Intracoastal Waterway.

History and Description: As mentioned in Chapter Two, I caught my first redfish on a fly rod using a deer hair popper. Of course, "deer hair popper" is contradiction in terms, because deer hair quickly waterlogs and sinks. To keep it afloat, I began to glue a fold of 2 mm closed cell foam in front of the deer hair body. But within two years, I changed the fold of foam to a trapezoidal block of form, and the pattern seemed complete. Since I introduced the pattern in *Fly Tyer* magazine, the VIP has appeared in several other national magazines, and has become quite popular among Texas fly fishers.

The VIP embodies several qualities that account for its effectiveness. It is lightweight and easy to cast in the wind, but it has a large profile for its weight. Hence it is quite visible. Also, the deer-hair breaks the surface film of the water and sits low on the surface. This keeps the popper from "waking out" as the fish rises to take it. The wide-gap, chemically sharpened Gamakatsu B10S hook rounds out the fly's list of virtues and accounts for a significantly higher percentage of hookups than a popper tied on a standard hooKathy

Tying Instructions:
Hook: Gamakatsu B10S #4 or #6
1) For the tail, tie in six to eight strands of Dupont Lumaflex, with a few strands of Crystal Flash.

2) Then, going forward, stack one bunch of deer body hair on top of hook, flare without spinning and wind forward through the hair for 1/4 inch, and then continue winding forward to the eye over the bare hook shanKathy Wind back and forth to build up thread base. Tie off and cut thread.

3) Prepare head from block of 6mm closed cell foam. Angle both front and back faces, so that block is shorter at bottom to fit the remaining hook shanKathy

4) Push bodkin needle through bottom of block, from back to front.

5) Remove bodkin needle from blocKathy

6) Push block over hook eye to make sure it fits and will slide

easily over the eye once the shank has glue on it.

7) Remove the head from the hook shanKathy

8) Put drop of Superglue on hook shanKathy

9) Again, push block over eye. Move back quickly against deer hair, making a tight seal. Trim deer hair.

10) Attach doll eyes with Superglue.

11) Add inline mono weedguard by heating bodkin needle and insert it behind the hook eye to make a hole for the guard.

12) Cut a piece of 20- to 30-pound mono, and insert into hole, such that the mono lines up and extends just outside the hook point. Add a drop of Superglue to anchor the weedguard.

The Mother's Day Fly

Uses: This fly is especially effective for sight casting to cruising trout after midmorning, once the sun is high in the sky.

History and Description: I first tied this fly in its current form in 2000, on the day before Mother's Day. I gave the fly to Kathy, and the next day she used it to catch the largest redfish that she'd ever caught on a fly rod to date. Just as the VIP evolved over a period of many years, the MDF went through several refinements before arriving at its current form. Even in '97, I was using a prototype of this fly for big trout. Since then, it has become my hands-down favorite subsurface fly for big trout and redfish alike. It performs beautifully — in the air and in the water, since it's lightweight and undulates as it sinks. Indeed, the fish often take it "on the drop" because of the legging material, which never stops moving.

The MDF features glass or bead-chain eyes either mounted at mid-shank, split saddle hackle tails, a body made from Estaz, palmered hackle, and two or four legs made from Dupont Lumaflex. The legs will help turn the fly over so that the hook will ride up and undulate even at rest. In water deeper than a foot, use glass or weighted eyes to sink the fly. I use glass beads attached by the "melted mono method" that I describe below, as they are a compromise between the weightlessness of plastic and the weight of brass or lead. White, pink, orange, and chartreuse are effective body colors, and I like barred olive for palmering and tails.

Tying Instructions:
Hook: Daichi 2546 size 4, or Gamakatsu SS15 size 4

1) Tie in a tuft of hot pink or chartreuse marabou to split the tails and serve as an attractor.

2) Then tie two saddles to each side of the tuft of marabou, so that they are effectively divided by the tuft. Let them extend behind the hook about 1.5 inches.

3) Tie in the Estaz body material, and a long barred olive saddle hackle that you will palmer through the body material.

4) For glass bead eyes: Go forward, and tie a piece of 40- to 50-pound mono across the hook one third of the way from the hook bend to the hook eye. Put a drop of Superglue on the wraps.

5) Thread a glass bead on either side to where the eyes lie against the hook shanKathy Light the mono on fire and let it burn into the opening of the glass eye. But before you light the mono, wrap your thread forward to avoid burning the thread. Put drop of Superglue on the inside of the beads to secure them further to the mono. Wrap the thread around the base of the eyes to ensure that they will remain stationery, and then put a drop of Superglue on the wraps.

6) Wrap the Estaz forward, and anchor with your tying thread. then palmer the long saddle forward and anchor.

7) Turn the hook over, and tie in a few strands of Lumaflex. Trim it to 1.5 inches.

8) Tie a short piece of stiff 30-pound mono just behind the hook eye so it stands angled backward.

9) Trim the mono to half an inch, and add a drop of Superglue, or head cement, to the wraps.

About the Author

G. Scott Sparrow, Ed.D. is an associate professor at the University of Texas-Rio Grande Valley, a charter faculty member at Atlantic University in Virginia Beach, a Licensed Professional Counselor in Texas, a Licensed Marriage and Family Therapist in Virginia, an FFF-certified fly casting instructor, and a saltwater fly fishing guide on the Lower Laguna Madre of deep south Texas. He currently practices psychotherapy at The Center in McAllen, Texas. He is an Advisor to the International Association for the Study of Dreams' Executive Committee, as well as an IASD Board member and past President. Scott's academic work can be found at www.dreamanalysistraining.com, and his flyfishing services can be accessed at www.lagunamadreflyfishing.com.